Sweden's Regional Recipes

Sweden's Regional Recipes

Orrefors Crystal Candleholders

Compiled by Diana Johnson Kia
Photography by Robert and Loren Paulson

Dedication and Acknowledgments

Many years ago I became acquainted with Ester Harkins, to whom this book is dedicated. I asked her to teach me the Swedish language and, fortunately for me, she agreed. Over the next ten years, Ester patiently led me through lesson books and on to discover great literary works, including novels like *The Wonderful Adventures of Nils* and *The Further Adventures of Nils Holgersson* by Selma Lagerlöf.

This knowledge has enriched my life in countless ways, and I am eternally grateful. Swedish author Selma Lagerlöf (1858–1940) wrote the two novels about the adventures of a boy named Nils who, magically transformed into a tiny "Tom Thumb," travels with a flock of wild geese on their annual migration across Sweden. Quotes from these books introduce each chapter of this book.

Next, thanks to my family in Sweden, especially my cousin Paul Wiberg, his wife, Gunilla, and daughter, Sara, for helping me get started. I am grateful to my new friend in Sweden, Barbro Halvorsson, for her help with research on the provinces, and to Margit Asterling for helping me track down regional specialties. Thanks also to my husband for his patience all these months as I sat immersed in notes and recipes, glued to the computer, and often, I fear, neglecting him. And, finally, to my parents, Leroy and Linnea Johnson, my grandmother Anna Elge, and the town of Stanton, Iowa, for fostering in me a deep appreciation of my Swedish heritage.

—*Diana Johnson Kia*

Editors: Joan Liffring-Zug Bourret, Maureen Patterson, Dorothy Crum, Charlotte Anderson, Marta Cullberg Weston, Miriam Canter, Esther Feske, Melinda Bradnan, and Dwayne Bourret

Photography: Robert and Loren Paulson

Drawings: Diane Heusinkveld and the late Helen Elizabeth Blanck, from her book *The Flowers of Dalarna,* courtesy Tom Blanck. Helen taught folk art for many years at the American Swedish Institute in Minneapolis.

ISBN 1-932043-19-5

CONTENTS

***Left:** Author Diana Johnson Kia is near the Dalarna-style coffee cup water tower, Stanton, Iowa, which also has a coffeepot tower. **Above:** Loren, left, and his father, Robert Paulson, both distinguished photographers, in Minneapolis, Minnesota.*

Diana writes, "I was born in Montana and lived much of my life in Chicago, but I have always considered Stanton, Iowa, my home. It's literally my home now, because my husband, a former Motorola executive, and I moved here at retirement. I worked for many years as a nurse and now in Stanton I write for the local newspaper. My parents were born here, and this is where I spent happy summers as a child, when there were many native-born Swedes in Stanton. Today, their descendants keep the heritage alive. Every summer *Svenska skolan* (Swedish school) is held for youngsters at our wonderful Swedish Heritage and Cultural Museum. We celebrate *Midsommar* and Santa Lucia Day, sing to welcome beautiful May, and hold an annual *lutfisk* supper."

For several decades Robert and Loren Paulson, father and son, have produced magnificent calendars showing their photographs of Scandinavian countries. They produce videos, books, and postcards and import heritage items through their Paulstad Communications.

Preface

In 1991 my husband and I made our first trip to Sweden, along with our daughter, Becky, and youngest son, David. I was excited about seeing the land of my ancestors and meeting relatives with whom I'd been corresponding, excited about introducing two of my children to their Swedish heritage, excited about my new video camera. I was excited about the trip in general, but not about food. Food wasn't high on my list of expectations. In fact, I barely gave it any thought at all.

Swedish cuisine came as a bonus, a delightful surprise to us all! My relatives treated us like royalty, and the meals they served in their homes were wonderful. At the home of my mother's cousin Asta Wiberg, David, eleven at the time and fussy about what he would and wouldn't eat, declared, "Asta is the best cook in the world!" I couldn't argue with him then, and I wouldn't now.

In restaurants, too, the meals were delicious, though pricey. Swedes don't eat out as often as Americans do, and when they do it's generally a special occasion, and they're willing to pay a bit more.

Sweden is a large country by European standards, with twenty-five provinces, similar to states or counties in the United States. Each province is unique in its history and character, and each has its own culinary specialties.

In Sweden today, as in America, people enjoy many types of foods, including Italian, Chinese, and Mexican dishes. They are also health conscious and tend to eat light. Recently, there has been a revival of interest in *husmanskost*, or "Good old down-home traditional Swedish cooking." Most of the recipes in this book fall into that category.

Swedish Table Prayer

I Jesu namn till bords vi gå;

Välsigna, Gud, den mat vi få.

Amen

Translation

In Jesus's name to the table we go;

Bless, O God, the food we receive.

Amen

Gustav Vasa's Confirmation Church Near Vaxholm

THE NORTHERN PROVINCES

LAPPLAND

"Onward, onward!" urged the sun as it climbed the steep cliffs. "There's no danger so long as I am with you."

—From *The Further Adventures of Nils Holgersson*
by Selma Lagerlöf

Lappland is the northernmost and largest province in Sweden. Renowned as the "land of the midnight sun," Lappland stretches far into the Arctic Circle. In midsummer the sun never sets, only dips close to the horizon around midnight and then begins to rise again. Winters here are correspondingly dark, long, and cold.

It's a high and rocky land, with broad expanses of tundra and pine forest populated by bear, wolf, lynx, ptarmigan, falcon, and many other types of wildlife. Sweden's deepest lake, Hornavan, and its highest mountain, Kebnekaise, are found here. Large deposits of iron ore have resulted in the growth of modern industrial centers, contributing greatly to the prosperity of the entire country. Mighty "iron mountains" rise above the thriving city of Kiruna, the largest city in Sweden — in area, not population. Kiruna is a young city, dating from 1900.

Away from the cities live the reindeer-herding native Lapplanders, who prefer to be called *Sami*. This name bears a similarity to the English word "same," and the *Sami* like to say that they consider themselves to have the same value as everyone else, neither more nor less.

Because of the sparse vegetation of the tundra, reindeer herds must move freely over their grazing grounds and so the *Sami* traditionally lived a nomadic lifestyle, moving their tents along as they followed their herds. Today they live in villages and herd their reindeer with the use of helicopters, snowmobiles, and walkie-talkies. Native dress is also gradually giving way to "western" style, though many still wear traditional garb, especially on special occasions.

The *Sami* folk are known for their colorful arts and crafts, called *duodji,* which provide them with a significant source of supplemental income. Items such as jewelry, knives, and tools made of silver, tin, wood, and reindeer antlers are displayed and sold in shops, museums, and at summer exhibitions.

Sami music, *yoiking,* is one of the most ancient forms of music in the world. These songs have been passed down from generation to generation, telling stories of man and nature. Originally, this music was also a form of worship, of communication with their many gods. Like Native Americans, the ancient *Sami* believed that everything in nature has a spirit, and even today they have great respect for the natural world.

Today there are approximately fifteen thousand *Sami* in Sweden, mostly in the northern provinces, another eighteen thousand in Norway, three thousand in Finland, and two thousand in Russia. They maintain their own language, culture, and traditions.

The *Sami* are an ethnic minority in Sweden and have at times been subject to prejudice and discrimination. In recent years things have improved for them. Their rights are legally safeguarded and their political influence is increasing.

Traditional cuisine in Lappland includes reindeer meat prepared in various ways, as well as game fowl and a special soft, flatbread called polar bread.

A Reindeer Rodeo

Reindeer Fillet *(Renfilé)*

1-1/2 pounds reindeer fillet
(may also use venison or beef)
salt and pepper
oil or margarine, divided
2 cups beef bouillon, divided
1 yellow onion, sliced
2 cups sliced mushrooms
1 cup *créme fraiche*
(or whipping cream)
1 teaspoon arrowroot (or other thickening agent like cornstarch)
chili sauce
lemon juice

Trim the fillet. Season with salt and pepper and brown in oil or margarine in a skillet. Baste with 1/2 cup bouillon and simmer slowly for about 15 to 20 minutes, depending on thickness. In a separate skillet, heat oil or margarine and sauté the onion and mushrooms until tender. Season with salt and pepper. Set aside and keep warm.

Slice the fillet into 1/2-inch slices and lay them on a serving platter. Dilute the pan drippings with remaining bouillon. Add the *créme fraiche*, bring to a boil, and thicken with arrowroot or cornstarch dissolved in a little water. Season with chili sauce, lemon juice, and salt and pepper. Pour the sauce over the meat and place the mushrooms and onions on the side. Serve with boiled potatoes and a green vegetable. Serves 6.

Reindeer Stroganoff *(Renskavspanna)*

1 pound reindeer steak
(may also use venison or beef)
salted water
flour
butter or margarine
1 cup chopped onions
1 cup sliced mushrooms
1 cup beef bouillon
10 juniper berries, crushed
1/2 teaspoon salt
1 teaspoon Worcestershire sauce
1 teaspoon soy sauce
1 cup sour cream

Soak meat in salted water overnight. Trim and cut into 1/2-inch strips. Roll in flour and brown in butter. Remove meat from pan and sauté onions and mushrooms. Add bouillon, juniper berries, salt, and sauces. Add meat. Cover and simmer slowly about 1 hour. Add cream just prior to serving and heat through. Serves 4.

Meat Stew *(Renragu)*

1 pound boneless reindeer meat
(may use venison or beef)
butter
2 leeks, sliced
2 celery stalks, chopped fine
2 tablespoons flour
1 teaspoon salt
1/2 teaspoon white pepper
1 teaspoon thyme
2 cups beef bouillon
1/2 cup cream

Cut the meat into 3/4-inch cubes. Brown the meat in butter and transfer to a saucepan. Brown the leeks and celery. Add to the meat. Sprinkle with flour. Season with salt, pepper, and thyme, then add the bouillon. Cover and simmer until the meat is tender, about 40 minutes. Add the cream and heat through. Serves 4.

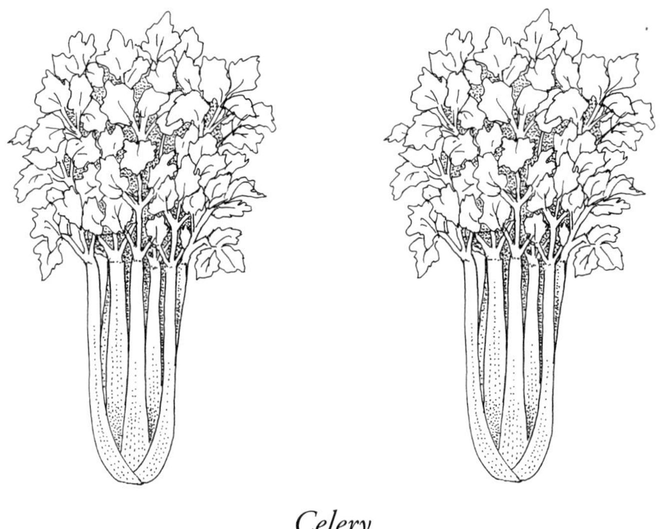

Celery

Ptarmigan *(Ripa)*

I have never seen a ptarmigan, but I used the following recipe for pheasant and got rave reviews from the self-appointed critics in my family! (Pheasant being a larger bird, I doubled the recipe.)

1 ptarmigan
salt and pepper
oil for browning
1/3 cup chicken-flavored bouillon
1/3 cup red wine
6 baby carrots (or two large carrots cut into thirds)
1/2 medium onion, cut into chunks
8 crushed juniper berries

Gravy ***(Sås)*****:**
pan drippings
2 tablespoons flour

Clean and dry the ptarmigan and sprinkle it with salt and pepper. Brown in oil in a frying pan, then transfer to a cooking pot. Baste with bouillon and red wine (or you may omit the wine and use 2/3 cup bouillon). Add carrots, onion, and crushed juniper berries to the pot. Cover and cook over very low heat for about 1-1/2 hours, until the legs may be easily loosened from the body. Remove the ptarmigan and the vegetables from the pot, set aside, and keep warm.

Strain the pan drippings and return them to the pot. Mix the flour with a little of the liquid, then stir this into the rest of the liquid to make the gravy. Simmer for a couple minutes. Season with salt and pepper.

Editor's Note: One ptarmigan serves just one person. A pheasant may be shared.

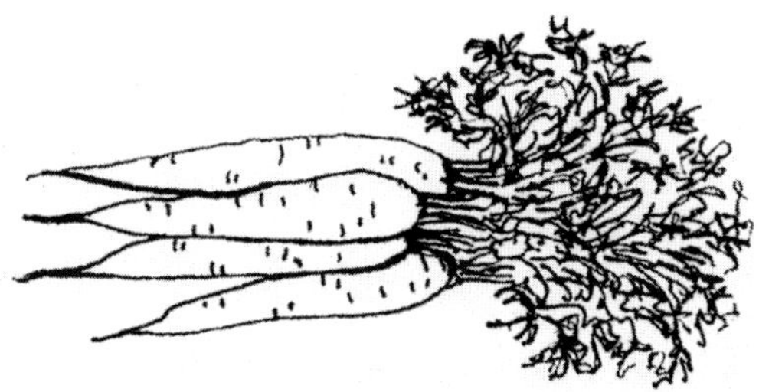

Carrots

Polar Bread *(Polarbröd)*

2 cups milk
2 packets yeast
1/4 cup molasses
1 teaspoon salt
1/2 teaspoon baking powder
1 cup sifted rye flour
2/3 cup barley flour
2-1/2 cups (approx.) white flour

Warm the milk until lukewarm; pour into a mixing bowl. Dissolve the yeast in the milk. Mix in molasses, salt, baking powder, and flour. Turn out dough onto a floured board and knead. (Add more white flour if necessary.) Return to the bowl, cover with a cloth, and allow to rise for 1 to 2 hours.

Preheat the oven to 450°. Turn the dough out again onto a floured surface. Knead the dough again and divide into eight approximately equal pieces. Roll out each piece into a thin circle. Prick all over with a fork. Place on a lightly greased baking sheet. Bake each piece until lightly browned, about 4 minutes. Fold the flatbreads and leave to cool covered with a cloth. Place in airtight container before they cool completely.

NORRBOTTEN AND VÄSTERBOTTEN

"Wild geese must learn to eat air and drink wind," said the leader goose, and kept right on flying.

—From *The Further Adventures of Nils Holgersson*
by Selma Lagerlöf

Norrbotten and Västerbotten lie to the east of Lappland. These provinces each have a long coastline on the Baltic Sea, and early residents of the area derived much of their income from fishing and seal hunting. Today, mining is the largest industry.

Piteå and Luleå are the largest cities in Norrbotten. Luleå is well known for its steelworks and also for the unique buildings of its *Gammelstaden,* or old town.

The valleys of Norrbotten are quite fertile, and harvests are plentiful despite the short summers. Some potatoes, rye, and barley are grown, but the main crop is hay, which is stored in picturesque barns that dot the landscape. Moose, grouse, and many kinds of waterfowl live in the vast forests. Fishing is still important. Whitefish are harvested by net each summer from the Torne river, and on the last Sunday of July, a "Whitefish Festival" is celebrated in the city of Kukkola. Today, Västerbotten is well known for its cheese.

Västerbotten is made up of three different types of landscape: coastline, forest, and mountains. In summer the low-lying eastern coastal lands are subject to flooding, and before the development of modern roads, travel on these boggy plains was very difficult. Most travel in those days was done in winter, by ski or sled.

The land rises gradually to the west, with forests of pine and fir covering the largest part of the province, and beyond them the mountains. Many rivers flow down from the mountains toward the sea, some harnessed for hydroelectric power.

The earliest inhabitants of the region lived primarily by fishing and seal hunting. Next came the eras of forestry, shipbuilding, and mining, while the *Sami* tended their reindeer herds. In 1867, as the number of settlements in the province grew, a "cultivation line" was established to protect *Sami* territory. As it turned out, the line has also protected settlers. Settlements are not to be built north of the line, while the *Sami* are required to keep their reindeer above the cultivation line from May 1 to October 1. During the winter they may bring the herds down to winter pasture.

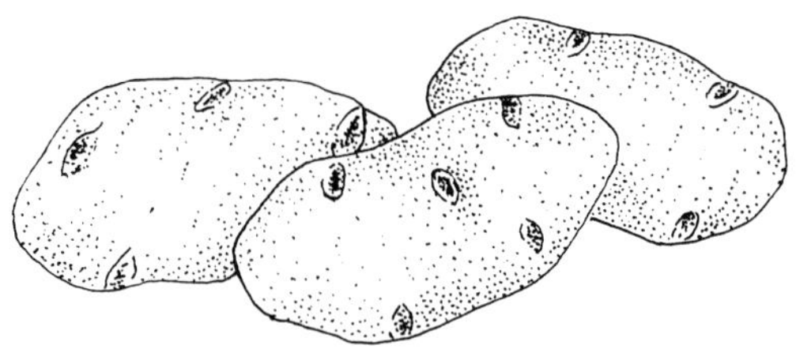

Potatoes

Piteå Potato Dumplings *(Pitepalt)*

One of the best known traditional dishes of the northern provinces is palt, *or potato dumplings—simple, hearty fare for those accustomed to an active life in the out-of-doors.*

When my daughter Becky was in fifth grade she began corresponding with a Swedish pen pal named Ylva Johansson. Their correspondence continued through the years and, in 1991, when both girls were twenty-five years old, they finally met in Sweden. The following two recipes for palt *were contributed by Ylva, now married with two children, who lives in the city of Piteå, Norrbotten.*

5 ounces lightly salted, precooked pork (add spices as desired, or use your favorite pork sausage)
6 medium-sized potatoes
1-1/2 teaspoons salt
1/3 cup corn flour
approx. 1 cup white flour

Set a large pot of water to boil. Add 2 teaspoons salt per quart of water. Chop or grind the pork into small pieces. Peel and grate the potatoes. Place them in a colander and press out the water. Mix the potatoes, salt, and flour into a dough. Use only as much flour as necessary to hold together.

Form about 1/2 cup of the dough into a ball with your hands. If you keep your hands wet it will be easier. Make a depression in the ball and fill it with 1 tablespoon pork; form the dough around and completely cover the meat. With a wet spoon, carefully place the ball into the boiling water. Repeat until all dough has been used. There should be about eight to twelve dumplings.

Gently loosen the dumplings from the bottom of the pot. Simmer for 45 minutes with the lid slightly open. Serve with butter and lingonberry jam. Serves 4.

Blood Dumplings *(Blodpalt)*

Here's a variation for the adventurous. I must admit that I haven't tried this one, but I can remember my great-aunt Ella and her husband, John Kindberg, whom I called "Grandpa," preparing it in their kitchen in Stanton, Iowa.

2 cups beef or pork blood
1 cup rye flour
2 teaspoons salt
1 teaspoon white pepper
1 quart cold, cooked, mashed potatoes
wheat flour
5 ounces precooked ground pork

Mix the blood, rye flour, salt, and pepper together, then allow the mixture to rise for about 2 hours. Add the mashed potatoes and enough wheat flour to make a workable dough. Make dumplings with pork centers as in potato dumplings, previous page, except boil for 60 minutes instead of 45.

On a Skiing Trip **(Pä skidtur)**

Illustrations above and right from Svenska Turistföreningens Årsskrift 1922

Whitefish in Cream Sauce *(Stuvad sik)*

2 pounds whitefish fillets
(or any mild, white fish)
1 teaspoon salt
2 tablespoons flour
3/4 cup water
2 tablespoons butter or margarine
1/2 cup chopped fresh dill
8 peppercorns, crushed
1/3 cup milk or cream
2 tablespoons lemon juice

Rinse and dry the fillets; sprinkle with salt. Mix the flour with a little of the water to a smooth consistency. Gradually add the rest of the water. Set aside. Melt the butter in a frying pan and lay the fish in the pan; sprinkle with dill and crushed pepper. Pour the flour/water mixture over all. Simmer 8 to 10 minutes. Add the cream and lemon juice and heat through.

NORTH-CENTRAL PROVINCES

ÅNGERMANLAND

The country west of him was all peaks and table land, and the farther away they were, the higher and wilder they looked.

—From *The Further Adventures of Nils Holgersson*
by Selma Lagerlöf

Traveling south to the province of Ångermanland one encounters a dramatic change of scenery. Here, instead of a low-lying, marshy coastline we find steep, rocky cliffs rising from the sea. This is known as Sweden's high coast *(Höga Kusten)*. At their highest points the cliffs rise 2,429 feet above the water, while offshore the ocean bottom dips 982 feet below the surface, and the islands of the archipelago jut sharply out of the water.

Here lie the Ulv Islands *(Ulvöarna),* which are famous not only for their unique cliff formations but also for their *surströmming,* (soured Baltic herring), a delicacy to many but definitely an acquired taste. The herring are canned and allowed to ferment for about a year, by which time the cans are bulging. When they are opened a pungent odor is released. The herring are usually eaten on pieces of thin crispbread, with new potatoes and raw yellow onion. *Surströmming* festivals are held in northern Sweden every autumn.

Ångermanland is sparsely populated, with most people living along the coast or in the river valleys. Five rivers come together here as they meet the sea. Their fertile banks are used for agriculture.

The province is covered with coniferous forest. Birch is one of the few deciduous trees able to thrive this far north. The climate varies from temperate at the coast to almost arctic inland, where winter lasts from October until early May.

Lumber and paper production is the region's main industry. Giant dam construction has also made this province a major exporter of electricity to the rest of Sweden.

Thin Crispbread *(Knäckebröd)*

You don't need surströmming *to enjoy this tasty crispbread. Try it with butter, cheese, tuna, chicken salad, or whatever you choose!*

2 packets yeast
2-1/4 cups water, lukewarm
2 teaspoons salt
1 cup rye flour
1 cup barley flour
1 cup oat flour
2 to 2-1/2 cups white flour
additional white flour as needed for rolling out

Dissolve the yeast in the lukewarm water. Add the salt and flour and work into a dough. Turn the dough out onto a board and knead. Cut into three parts. Cut each of these into four parts so that you now have twelve and form each part into a ball. Cover and allow to rise in a warm place for about an hour. With no further kneading, roll each ball into a very thin circle, then prick all over the surface with a fork or roll with a knobbed rolling pin. Place on a lightly greased or sprayed baking pan. (You will need to handle the thin dough like pie crust as you transfer it.) Bake at 425° for 6 to 8 minutes. Allow to cool uncovered.

The crispbread may be served as is or cut into cracker-sized squares or rectangles.

Baking Bread at a Folk Museum

The following two recipes were provided by Börje Eriksson of the Gudmundrå Home District Association in Ångermanland. I have altered the instructions slightly to reflect my own experience when trying this out. We found it quite tasty.

"Stirred" Cheese Pudding *(Rörost)*

2 quarts milk
1 rennet tablet (the type for cheese, not the type for ice cream), crushed and dissolved in 1 tablespoon water
1/4 cup sugar
1 teaspoon cinnamon
1 teaspoon cardamom
1 tablespoon flour mixed with 1/2 cup milk

Warm the milk to lukewarm (98°), stir in the rennet, pour into a large mixing bowl, and set aside for 45 minutes until it sets. Cut through three or four times in both directions with a knife; allow to set for another 45 minutes.

Carefully transfer to a colander and drain off 16 ounces of whey; discard. Return soft curd to the saucepan. Stir in the sugar, cinnamon, and cardamom and place the pot over low heat again. After it has simmered for a few minutes, drain off the remaining whey. Stir the flour/milk mixture into the cheese. Bring to a boil once more. Serve warm or cold, plain or topped with fruit.

Lingonberry Dessert Drink *(Vattenlingon)*

According to Börje, this is a tried-and-true dessert drink that is easy to prepare. It should be made during berry season and, if well-preserved, can be enjoyed all winter long.

lingonberries
water
sugar (optional)
whipped cream (optional)
ice cream (optional)

Fill clean wine bottles with lingonberries. Add water that has been boiled and allowed to cool. Fill the bottles up to the necks, then cork and store them on their sides, as you would wine.

Before serving, sweeten with sugar, according to taste. A dab of whipped cream or ice cream in the glass are other tasty options.

MEDELPAD

He heard the boy remark to himself that in a country like [this] ... it must be impossible for people to live. ... When the eagle heard the boy's remark, he replied: "Up here they have forests for fields."

—From *The Further Adventures of Nils Holgersson*
by Selma Lagerlöf

Forestry was once the primary industry in Medelpad. In old Swedish, *medelpad* means "the land between the rivers" and two rivers, the Indalsälven and the Ljungan, have always been vital to the region. Once, they provided the only means of transport for lumber, a task now accomplished mainly by trucks and trains. Today, the rivers are an important source of hydroelectric power.

Sweden's energy policy aims to reduce dependence on petroleum and gradually phase out nuclear power production altogether. The country is looking toward energy sources that are plentiful, renewable, and environmentally safe, including solar and water power.

In addition to their practical value, the rivers are also scenic, and provide great fishing. Arctic trout is a favorite catch.

For sea fishing, many tourists visit Alnö, an island off the coast, where they also may enjoy swimming and sightseeing. The north side of the island is well known for its unique geology, with rocks and minerals not found in any other part of Sweden and in few other places in the world. A volcanic eruption around 500 million years ago brought to the surface more than seventy different types of minerals. Rich and beautiful plant life also flourishes here.

Arctic Trout *(Röding)*

I used rainbow trout for this recipe, and they turned out very well.

4 trout, about 8 ounces each
white pepper
2 teaspoons salt, divided
3 tablespoons butter or margarine
1/4 cup water
1-1/8 cups milk or cream
2 tablespoons minced chives

Rinse the fish; pat dry. Sprinkle inside and out with pepper and 1 teaspoon salt. Fry the fish over medium-low heat in butter or margarine for 5 to 7 minutes on each side, until cooked through. Place the fish on a platter and keep warm while preparing the sauce.

To make sauce: Pour the water into the same frying pan used for the fish and bring to a boil. Add the milk, chives, and 1 teaspoon salt. Stir constantly while it returns to a boil, then reduce heat and simmer for 3 to 5 minutes, stirring occasionally. Drizzle sauce over fish just before serving. Serves 4.

JÄMTLAND AND HÄRJEDALEN

"It's called Härjedalen, Härjedalen," crowed the rooster. "How does it look down there where you are?" the boy asked. "Cliffs in the west, woods in the east, broad valleys across the whole country," replied the rooster.

—From *The Further Adventures of Nils Holgersson*
by Selma Lagerlöf

Jämtland and Härjedalen together are sometimes called "Europe's last wilderness." Tourists come from all over the world. The landscape is breathtaking, with high mountains, waterfalls, and rivers that provide canoeing and fishing in the summer and downhill skiing in the winter.

Rock carvings scattered around the provinces, dating back to 3000 BC, depict hunting scenes. In those days, moose hunting involved carving pits into which the animals would fall. Many of these pits remain. On a cliff wall in western Härjedalen are giant drawings, dating back 4,000 years, of reindeer, moose, and bear.

Plenty of these animals still roam the woods, as well as lynx, wolverines, and other less-fearsome kinds of wildlife. Moose hunting remains popular here as in most of Sweden, although hunters no longer dig pits. They often work in teams, with two or three *drevkarlar* (drivers), walking through the forest, driving the game toward those who wait with guns. Hunting is strictly regulated, with limits on how much game may be taken.

One of the area's most famous "animals" is hunted only by camera. Jämtland's Storsjön (Great Lake) is rumored to be the home of *Storsjöodjuret*, or the sea monster. The story goes back about four hundred years, and since 1635 there have been claims of sightings by more than five hundred people. Move over, Nessie (the Scottish monster), you've got company!

The northernmost runestone in Sweden stands on Frösön (Frey's Island) near an ancient castle. A runestone is a rock, from Viking times, carved with letters of the ancient Norse alphabet. The Frösön stone is about one thousand years old and the inscription says, among other things, "Östman Gudfast's son Christianized Jämtland." Jämtland has been part of Sweden since 1645; before that it belonged to Norway.

Östersund, the only large city in Jämtland or Härjedalen, was founded in 1786, but never really prospered until 1879, when a railroad was built. Since that time, tourism has become the primary industry.

Visitors to these provinces will surely enjoy trying *älgkött* (moose meat) and *äppelris* (apple rice pudding).

Child with the Beautiful Wildflowers of Sweden

Marinated Pot Roast of Moose *(Surstek på älg)*

My Aunt Asta Wiberg served us moose meat in Sweden, and it was delicious! If you can't get your hands on any, try this recipe with beef.

2 pounds boneless moose, such as bottom round

Marinade *(Marinad)*:

2 red onions
10 allspice berries
10 white peppercorns
3 to 4 bay leaves
1 bottle (approx. 3 cups) red wine
1/2 cup red wine vinegar
1/2 cup olive oil

For Braising *(Till bräsering)*:

butter or margarine
1 teaspoon salt
3/4 cup marinade
3/4 cup water

Gravy *(Sås)*:

1-1/2 cups braising juices
3 tablespoons flour
1/4 cup water
1/2 cup cream
salt and pepper

Place the meat in a deep pot. Peel and slice the onions; lightly crush the spices. Spread the onion and spices over the meat. Mix the wine, vinegar, and oil and pour over the meat. Cover completely. Refrigerate 7 to 10 days, turning occasionally.

Drain and dry the meat. Strain the marinade and set it aside. Brown the meat in butter on all sides in a roasting pan. Sprinkle with salt. Add the 3/4 cup marinade and 3/4 cup water. Cover and cook over low heat for 1-1/2 hours or until tender. Add more liquid if needed. Remove the roast to a serving platter and keep warm.

Strain the drippings and add enough water to make 1-1/2 cups. Heat to boiling.

Mix the flour and water and whip it into the gravy. Add the cream. Simmer for about 5 minutes. Season with salt and pepper. Serves 6.

Onions

Smoked Moose with Salad and Potatoes
(Rökt älgstek med sallad och potatis)

Here is the kind of light, low-fat meal favored by many of today's health-conscious Swedes.

4 baking potatoes
1 cup cottage cheese
1/4 cup light sour cream
salt
white pepper
garden cress or chopped parsley
1 pound smoked moose

Salad *(Sallad)*:
4 cups mixed greens
1 fresh cucumber, sliced
1 cup fresh mushrooms, sliced
2 tablespoons balsamic vinegar
2 tablespoons water
sprinkle of herb seasoning

Wash and pierce the potatoes, then bake at 400° for about an hour. Mix the cottage cheese with the sour cream, salt, and pepper. When the potatoes are done, cut them open and fill with the stuffing. Top with chopped garden cress or parsley.

Toss the salad ingredients together. Cut the meat into thin slices and serve with the baked potatoes and salad. Serves 4.

Apple Rice Dessert *(Äppelris)*

Adapted from the Swedish Dairy Institute

4 cups water
3/4 cup uncooked white rice
1 cinnamon stick
3 to 4 apples
whipped cream or non-dairy whipped topping

Bring water to a boil; add the rice and cinnamon stick. Simmer, covered, for 20 minutes. Peel, core, and slice the apples. Add them to the pot and allow to simmer until soft, about 10 more minutes. Drain off the water. Serve warm or cold, with whipped topping. Serves 4.

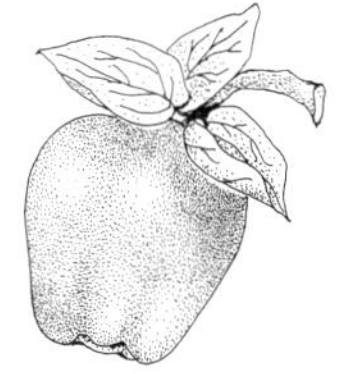
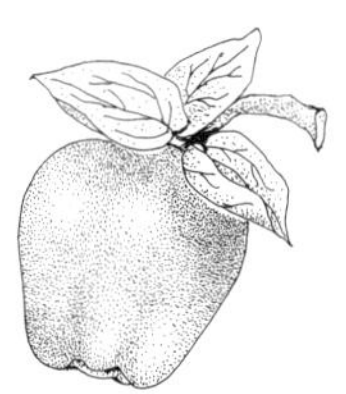

HÄLSINGLAND

It was a picturesque country to look down upon, and the boy saw a good deal of it.

—From *The Further Adventures of Nils Holgersson*
by Selma Lagerlöf

Hälsingland is characterized by many peninsulas, "necks" of land, along the coast. *Halsar* means necks and may account for the name of the province. The entire landscape is covered with moraine, rocks, and sediment deposited by glaciers.

There's a long history of travel and trade in Hälsingland, where in ancient times canals were dug to facilitate commercial travel to Norway. The Vikings of this area also had contact with the Far East, as evidenced by a sunken treasure of Arabian coins discovered in the Bay of Alfta.

During the sixteenth and seventeenth centuries, many Finnish immigrants came to Hälsingland. Several villages bear the names of those Finns, and examples of their craftsmanship can be found in homes and shops around the province.

The production of flax, wool, and woven fabric, as well as the timber industry, are important to the region's economy.

A culinary specialty of Hälsingland is the *sotare* (pronounced soot´aree, it means "chimney sweep"). This is a herring fried on the embers of an open fire, and traditionally served with boiled red potatoes and low-alcohol juniper beer. Another old-time favorite is barley cake.

Blackened Herring *(Sotare)*

2 pounds fresh herring
(or smelt or sardine)
1-1/2 teaspoons salt
juniper twigs soaked in water

Clean and rinse the fish and pat dry with a paper towel. Sprinkle inside and out with salt and refrigerate 2 to 3 hours. Light the barbeque and, when the coals are ready, cover them loosely with a layer of wet juniper twigs. Oil the grill or spray with nonstick cooking spray. Place the fish on the grill and broil about 2 minutes on each side, until cooked through.

Juniper Beer *(Enbärsdricka)*

2 pounds juniper twigs
and needles
10 quarts water
1 to 1-1/2 pounds sugar
1-3/4 ounces yeast

Place the twigs and needles in a cloth sack and boil for 1 hour and 15 minutes. Remove the bag and discard. Stir the sugar into the water and return to a boil for a minute or two. Allow to cool to 95°, then add the yeast. Cover and let stand 24 hours, unrefrigerated. Strain and bottle the brew. It will keep for about 2 weeks.

Poor Man's Barley Cake *(Fattigmans korngrynskaka)*

The following recipe will make a small batch of barley cake, just enough to cook in your double boiler.

4 ounces barley flour
1 cup water
2-1/4 cups milk
1/2 medium-sized onion, chopped
bacon, 1 or 2 strips, fried and cut into pieces
1/2 teaspoon salt
1 tablespoon syrup or honey

Place the flour in a bowl and gradually add the water and milk; stir in the onion, bacon, salt, and sweetening. Cook in the double boiler for about an hour, stirring occasionally. (It will become quite thick.)

Pour the mixture into a shallow oven dish that has been sprayed with nonstick spray and bake at 375° for about an hour. Remove from oven and allow to cool. Turn out of the oven dish onto a platter while still slightly warm. Cut the cake into pieces, fry, and serve with pork and mashed berries.

Harvesting Grain in Sweden

CENTRAL PROVINCES

GÄSTRIKLAND

"This country is clad in a spruce skirt and a gray stone jacket," thought the boy. "But around its waist it wears a girdle ... embroidered with blue lakes and green groves."

—From *The Further Adventures of Nils Holgersson*
by Selma Lagerlöf

The province of Gästrikland may be seen as the dividing line between the north and south of Sweden. Nature itself seems to emphasize this contrast. The western and northwestern parts of the region contain forests, hills, lakes, and rivers that are typically northern. In the eastern and southern parts of the province one finds fertile fields and boulder ridges common to the south of Sweden.

Iron ore is abundant in the western mountains. The history of mining in this region goes back to about AD 100 when, with primitive equipment and hard labor, the people made their province one of the largest iron producers in northern Europe. Iron played a very important role during the Viking Age, and during the seventeenth century iron became a major export industry. Today, the steel industry is well developed.

The most important city in Gästrikland is Gävle, which has grown from a fishing village and regional marketplace into a busy port. Over the years, fire has destroyed Gävle four times. The last fire, in 1869, made eight thousand of its ten thousand inhabitants homeless. The city was rebuilt with wide boulevards and large green areas and parks, intended to prevent this from ever happening again.

My friend Barbro tells me that there is a custom in Gävle that every year at Christmastime a giant *julbock* (Christmas goat made of straw) is erected in the middle of the town square. A Web camera is trained on the *bock* and one can check on it daily by Internet. After the holidays, someone customarily sets fire to it. This is expected and tolerated. But one recent Christmas an American tourist set fire to the *bock* before Christmas. He was arrested and taken in for questioning. He claimed someone had played a trick on him, telling him this was the tradition. Local citizens were probably doubtful.

Fried Baltic Herring *(Stekt strömming)*

Baltic herring are plentiful off the coast of Gästrikland, and every year in May, Strömmingens Dag *(Herring Day) is celebrated.*

2-1/4 pounds baltic herring
(smelt may be used instead)
1/2 cup bread crumbs
1-1/2 teaspoons salt
1/4 teaspoon pepper
2 tablespoons butter or margarine

Cut the herring into chunks. Rinse and dry. Mix the bread crumbs with the salt and pepper, and dip the fish into this mixture to coat.

Heat the butter in a frying pan. Fry the fish over moderate heat about 3 to 5 minutes on each side. Serves 4.

Lingonberry Rice *(Lingonris)*

Adapted from the Swedish Dairy Institute

2/3 cup uncooked rice
4 cups water, boiling
2 tablespoons sugar
1 tablespoon grated lemon peel
3/4 cup whipping cream
1 teaspoon vanilla extract
2/3 cup lingonberry preserves

Cook the rice in the boiling water 25 to 30 minutes. Drain and allow to cool. Mix the sugar and grated lemon peel into the rice. Whip the cream until stiff and then stir in the vanilla. Mix with the rice.

Spread half the rice mixture in a serving bowl, then the lingonberries, and top with the remaining rice. Chill well before serving. Serves 4 to 6.

DALARNA

Coming generations would know their forefathers had been a good and wise folk, and they would remember them with reverence and gratitude.

—From *The Further Adventures of Nils Holgersson*
by Selma Lagerlöf

Dalarna, located in the center of the country, is considered by many the "heart of Sweden" with its rich traditions, colorful folk costumes, arts, and crafts. Perhaps it is because of the work of two artists, Carl Larsson and Anders Zorn, that images of this province have become, to many, the very image of Sweden itself.

In the center of Dalarna is beautiful Lake Siljan. In olden days churches were built around the edge of the lake, and people went to worship on Sundays in long rowboats that traveled along the shoreline picking up passengers. Nowadays tourists enjoy riding in these boats and watching the rowing competitions held every summer.

The primary industries of Dalarna are tourism, handcrafts, and copper, silver, and iron mining. The great copper mine at Falun is considered a national treasure and is a major tourist attraction. It is known to have been in operation as early as the year 1000. During the sixteenth century, when Sweden was a great world power, the Falun copper mine produced 70 percent of the world's copper. The mine closed in 1992, but pigment from the red ochre in the mine is still produced on an industrial scale and is used to paint the characteristic red houses and barns across the countryside.

Arts, crafts, music, and theater all thrive here, both traditional and modern. Perhaps the best-known craft item is the *dalahäst,* a cheerful little wooden horse, usually red-orange or some other bright color, decorated with flowers and swirls. About four hundred thousand of these horses are produced each year, 20 percent for export. The world's largest *dala* horse stands in Avesta, Dalarna's southernmost city. It is more than 42 feet high and weighs 6.7 tons.

The people of Dalarna take great pride in preserving their heritage, as witnessed by the fact that one in every twelve inhabitants belongs to some local historical society. Traditional costume is worn here more frequently than in other provinces, especially for festive occasions like *Midsommar.* Dalarna is also known for wonderful food, including traditional dishes like *Falukorv* (Falu sausage) and *mandelformar med blåbär* (blueberry tartlets).

Falu Sausage *(Falukorv)*

This basic recipe was contributed by Hans Bengtsson of Dalarna and adapted for our use by Becky Jones of the Johnson Meat Locker of Essex, Iowa.

5 pounds ground beef
5 pounds lean pork
5 pounds fat pork
1 pound minced onion
4 ounces salt
1 tablespoon white pepper
1 to 2 teaspoons ginger
1 to 2 teaspoons nutmeg
10 pounds potatoes, peeled, diced, and blanched
sausage casings

Mix all ingredients well. Stuff the casings. Allow the sausages to dry somewhat and then smoke them lightly. The sausage should reach a temperature of 160° F, then quickly cool the sausage to 40° F.

Blueberry Tartlets *(Mandelformar med blåbär)*

Other fruits may be used, such as strawberries, raspberries, or cherries. I like to use some of each for a festive, colorful presentation.

Pastry *(Smördeg)*:
1/2 cup soft butter or margarine
1/4 cup sugar
1 egg white
1/2 teaspoon almond extract
1 cup sifted flour
3/4 cup blanched almonds, ground

Fruit Topping *(Frukt)*:
3 cups fresh blueberries
lemon leaves

Cream Filling *(Vaniljkräm)*:
1/4 cup sugar
1 tablespoon cornstarch
1 cup milk
2 egg yolks
3/4 teaspoon vanilla extract

Glaze *(Glasyr)*:
1 (3-ounce) package lemon gelatin
1-1/2 cups water

Preheat oven to 375°. In a medium bowl, combine the butter and sugar. Beat in the egg white. Add the almond extract, flour, and ground almonds. Use hands to mix this; it will be very stiff.

Line small tartlet tins with the dough. Place the tins on a cookie sheet and bake for 10 minutes or until light golden brown. Cool in tins for 10 minutes and then turn out.

To make the cream filling: Combine the sugar, cornstarch, and milk in a small saucepan. Bring to a boil over medium heat. Remove from heat and beat the egg yolks in quickly. Stir in the vanilla extract. Cool. Refrigerate, covered, overnight.

To make the glaze: Dissolve gelatin in boiling water. Chill until semi-set. (Prepare a few hours before serving.)

To serve: Place one spoonful of chilled cream into each pastry shell. Top with blueberries. Spoon a little glaze over each tartlet and chill until fully set. Garnish with lemon leaves.

Blueberries

VÄRMLAND

"I don't think I've ever seen the earth beneath us as lovely!" he finally remarked. "The lakes are like blue satin bands."

—From *The Further Adventures of Nils Holgersson*
by Selma Lagerlöf

Värmland is a large province in the center of Sweden that borders Norway on the west and Lake Vänern on the south. It is a province of long-established wealth, reflected in the magnificent architecture of its cities. Trade across the border with Norway has always been brisk, and the discovery of iron and other ores in the fifteenth century led to a booming mining industry. Ruins of the earliest ironworks can still be seen in the valley of Klarälven.

Värmland residents are proud of their beautiful landscape, with its many recreational opportunities. The high mountains, deep forests, and many lakes and streams are perfect for hiking, biking, canoeing, fishing, and other leisure pursuits.

One of Värmland's most famous natives is the author Selma Lagerlöf, who wrote the *Nils Holgersson* stories from which we have quoted throughout this book.

Each year at the beginning of February, a large motor-sport competition called the International Swedish Rally is held deep in the forests of Värmland. The city of Ransäter hosts two annual events: a folk music festival in June and an accordion festival in July.

Also each July, "Viking Week" is celebrated in the villages of Arvika and Säffle. This celebration commemorates the journey of a Viking king, Olof Trätälja, who once traveled across the province on his way to Norway seeking a bride. One can imagine that somewhere along his journey, Olof might have been treated to *Värmlandskorv med rotmos* (Värmland sausage with mashed turnips), a truly regal meal. Too bad chocolate wasn't invented until the 1400s or he might have topped it off with *Värmländsk chokladefterrätt* (Värmland's chocolate dessert).

Värmland Sausage with Rutabaga
(Värmlandskorv med rotmos)

The first time I made rotmos *my family was surprised at how much they liked it! We enjoy this dish not only with sausage, but also as an accompaniment to other meat entrées.*

Sausage ***(Korv)*****:**
6 pounds white potatoes
(about 10 large or 15 medium)
1 large onion
4 pounds ground pork
(not too lean)
white pepper to taste
10 to 12 feet of sausage casings
1-1/2 tablespoons salt

Rotmos**:**
1-1/2 pounds rutabaga
or yellow turnips
3 medium carrots
6 potatoes
6 cups water or milk
1 tablespoon butter or margarine
salt and pepper to taste
3 tablespoons chopped parsley

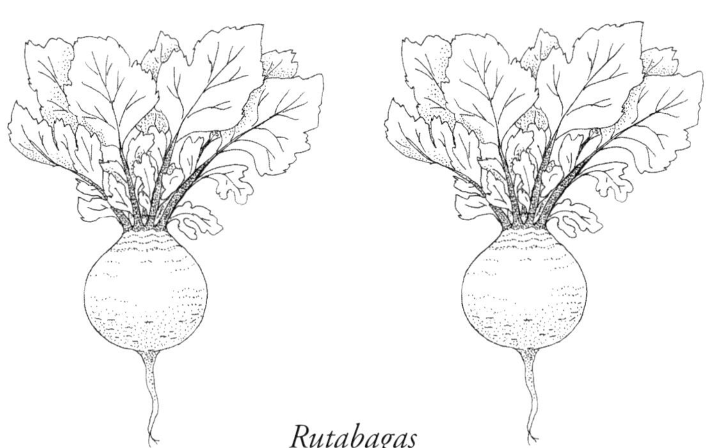

Rutabagas

Sausage: Peel and grate the raw potatoes and mince the onion. Mix the potatoes, onion, ground meat, and pepper together well. Stuff loosely into the casings. Cut off and tie in lengths of about 12 to 18 inches. Form into rings. Rub the sausages with salt and refrigerate overnight.

Rinse the sausages. Place two or three at a time into a large pot, cover with water, and boil for 45 minutes. (May be stored frozen, either before or after boiling.)

Rotmos: Peel and slice the rutabaga or yellow turnips, carrots, and potatoes. Bring the water to a boil. Add the rutabaga and carrots and boil for 20 minutes, then add the potatoes and continue boiling until done, about 20 to 30 minutes more. Drain the water, but save a little for thinning the mash. Purée the vegetables, thinning if needed. Add the butter. Season with salt and pepper and sprinkle with chopped parsley. Serve sausage and *rotmos* separately. Serves 8 to 10.

Värmland Dessert *(Värmländsk efterätt)*

Adapted from the Swedish Dairy Institute

1 cup butter or margarine
1-1/2 cups bread crumbs
  or graham cracker crumbs
2 tablespoons cocoa
3/4 cup whipping cream
3/4 cup strawberry preserves
fresh strawberries (optional)
chocolate chips or flakes
  (optional)

Melt the butter and mix with the bread crumbs and cocoa. Whip the cream. Alternate layers of bread-crumb mixture, preserves, and whipped cream in a bowl or individual serving dishes. (Glass bowls are nice, so you can see the layers.) Top with a dab of whipped cream and a strawberry, or a sprinkle of chocolate chips or flakes. Serves 4 to 6.

Strawberry

VÄSTMANLAND

"I'm reminded of the iron molders in the mining districts, who juggle with fire as if it were perfectly harmless," remarked the boy.

—From *The Further Adventures of Nils Holgersson*
by Selma Lagerlöf

Västmanland is one of Sweden's most industrialized provinces. Iron has been produced here since the fourteenth century, and a gunpowder factory operated in Gyttorp from 1858 until 1967. Today the Nitro Nobel Company, founded by Alfred Nobel, is Gyttorp's biggest industry.

The province has a long and impressive history. A collection of monuments dating from AD 800 to 1050, including gravestones set out in the shape of Viking longboats, can be seen near the city of Långby. The *reformationsriksdag* (reformation parliament) was held here in 1527 in connection with the declaration of Lutheranism as the official state religion. Castles and cathedrals bear witness to the important status of Sweden throughout the seventeenth century.

The landscape of this province is full of contrast, with many different types of plant and animal life. Deer, moose, beavers, and hedgehogs can be found, as well as hazel hens. Pike, perch, bass, trout, and salmon swim in the lakes and rivers.

Seasonal events in Västmanland include an international horse show in May and Grand National horse racing at what many consider Sweden's most beautiful racetrack in June. After an exhilarating, or perhaps disappointing, day at the races, why not celebrate or console oneself with a delicious dinner of meatballs and gravy, topped off with apple pancakes?

Meatballs and Gravy *(Köttbullar med gräddsås)*

2 pounds lean ground beef
1 pound lean ground pork
2 eggs, beaten
1/2 cup milk
1 cup mashed potatoes
1 cup dry bread crumbs
1 tablespoon brown sugar
2 teaspoons salt
1/2 teaspoon each: pepper, nutmeg, cloves, and allspice
flour
2 cups cream

Combine all ingredients except flour and cream. Roll into small balls and roll the balls in flour. Brown meatballs in oil in a frying pan, then transfer to a baking dish, pouring cream over the meatballs. Bake at 325° for an hour.

Apple Pancakes *(Äppelpannkaka)*

Adapted from the Swedish Dairy Institute

3/4 cup flour
1/2 teaspoon salt
2 cups milk, divided
3 eggs
1 tablespoon melted butter
4 apples
2 tablespoons sugar
1 teaspoon cinnamon
whipped cream

Mix the flour, salt, and a little of the milk. Whip to a smooth consistency. Mix in the rest of the milk, the eggs, and the melted butter. Core, peel, and slice the apples very thin. Mix the apple slices with the sugar and cinnamon in a small bowl.

Grease and preheat a frying pan. Spoon enough of the batter in to make a 10-inch circle. Spread a little of the apple slice mixture over the pancake. Allow to bake. Flip and bake the pancake on the other side. Repeat until batter and apple slices are all used. Serve with a little whipped cream. Serves 4.

UPPLAND

"Still the best thing about the province is not its beauty," [said he]. "Then what is it that's best?" asked the oarsman. "That it has always been a respected and honored province."

—From *The Wonderful Adventures of Nils*
by Selma Lagerlöf

Long before the city of Stockholm rose to prominence, the castles of the great kings of Svealand, as Sweden was called in those days, were located in Old Uppsala in the province of Uppland, and it was here that coronation ceremonies were held.

The great church of Old Uppsala burned down during the twelfth century, and the archbishop moved his headquarters to Uppsala, where his gothic cathedral still stands. The proclamation of the Swedish reformation was issued in Uppsala.

In 1574 a royal scandal occurred. King Erik XIV, in a fit of insane jealousy, committed what were called "the Sture murders." This led to an insurrection that placed Erik's half-brother Johan III on the throne while Erik was imprisoned at Örbyhus Castle. Legend has it that three years later, Erik, still in prison, was poisoned with pea soup by his enemies, who feared he would retake the throne. Pea soup is still served at Örbyhus, and those who are brave enough to try say it is delicious!

World-famous Uppsala University, founded in 1477, is the oldest university in the Nordic countries. Today it attracts students from all over the world and has an enrollment of 37,000.

One of Uppland's most famous people is the botanist Carl von Linné, who developed a system of classification for plants and animals still used today, after more than two hundred years. Linné himself traveled all over Sweden and sent his followers to travel the world, categorizing flora and fauna. They brought back many specimens of plant life, and in 1745 Linné supervised the reconstruction of the botanical garden at Uppsala University to house them. Visitors are welcome there, as well as at Linné's home, Hammarby, which is situated in a lovely garden outside Uppsala.

Pea Soup *(Ärtsoppa)*

2 tablespoons butter or margarine
1 pound stew meat, cut into small pieces
1 leek (white part), sliced
1 onion, chopped
2 carrots, cut into small chunks
10- to 12-ounce rutabaga or yellow turnip, chopped
1 teaspoon salt
1/4 teaspoon pepper
1 to 2 bay leaves
10 cups water
1 pound dry green or yellow split peas
2 medium-sized potatoes, peeled and cut into chunks

Melt the butter in a pot, brown the meat, add the leek and onion, and cook until soft. Add the carrots, rutabaga, and spices. Cover with water and bring to a boil. Simmer for 20 minutes.

Add the peas and potatoes. Simmer for another 30 minutes, or until peas and potatoes are soft.

Publisher's note:

King Gustav III (1742–1792) decreed that Swedes and Finns eat pea soup every Thursday. Swedes have dutifully been serving pea soup with pancakes for over three hundred years.

Author Diana Kia says this pea soup is one of her favorite recipes in this collection. Diana's recipe is unusual in calling for rutabaga or yellow turnips, carrots, and potatoes, making this pea soup more of a vegetable soup. Some recipes call for smoked port hocks, with carrots, celery, and onions; others list salted side pork or pork shoulder meat. A favorite pea soup recipe in Minnesota includes ham bone or ends of baked ham.

Marta Cullberg Weston writes that university students in Sweden traditionally serve a Swedish arrack liqueur known as *punsch* with the pea soup.

Peas

Beef with Horseradish Sauce *(Pepparrotskött)*

2 pounds chuck roast
6 cups water
1-1/2 teaspoons salt
2 medium-sized onions
2 carrots
2 parsnips
2 stalks celery
12 whole allspice

Sauce:
2 tablespoons butter or margarine
2 tablespoons flour
1 cup reserved beef broth
1 cup cream or milk
2 tablespoons grated horseradish
salt and pepper to taste

Place the meat in a kettle and cover with water. Add salt. Bring to a boil and skim. Cut the vegetables into chunks. Add them to the pot, return to a boil, and skim again. Add the allspice. Simmer for 1-1/2 to 2 hours or until done. Remove the meat and vegetables from the pot. Keep warm until ready to serve. Strain liquid and save 1 cup of the broth.

To make the sauce: Melt the butter in a saucepan, add flour, and stir until smooth and lump-free. Gradually add the reserved broth and cream, stirring constantly. Simmer for about 10 minutes, stirring occasionally. Remove from heat. Stir in the horseradish and seasoning.

Slice the meat and place on a platter along with the vegetables. Serve with boiled potatoes and warm horseradish sauce. Serves 6.

The Uppsala Cathedral

Apple Pie *(Äppelpaj)*

6 to 8 cooking apples
2 unbaked 9-inch pastry crusts
3/4 cups sugar
1/2 teaspoon cinnamon
2 tablespoons flour
pinch of salt
1 tablespoon lemon juice
2 tablespoons margarine

Peel, core, and slice the apples. Line a 9-inch pie plate with one crust and fill with sliced apples. Sprinkle with sugar, cinnamon, flour, salt, and lemon juice. Dot with margarine. Cover with the second crust, seal the edge all around, and prick to ventilate. Bake at 400° for 45 minutes.

Note: For a pastry recipe, see Baked Apples, page 51.

Tomb of Gustav Vasa, Uppsala Cathedral

SOUTH CENTRAL PROVINCES

SÖDERMANLAND

"It's not worthwhile to be sad, Nils Holgersson," said the sun. "This is a beautiful world to live in, both for big and little."

—From *The Further Adventures of Nils Holgersson*
by Selma Lagerlöf

Many believe that the first people to inhabit Sweden lived in the area of Södermanland. Fertile fields supported agriculture, and transportation was relatively easy on the many waterways connecting peaceful Lake Mälaren with the Baltic Sea.

Södermanland (the name is often shortened to "Sörmland") is located just to the south and west of the city of Stockholm, and as the city grew in size and importance, many members of the aristocracy chose to settle here. Their estates prospered, thanks to the rich agricultural land and easy access to Stockholm markets. Many of their manor houses and castles remain, as well as some from before the time Stockholm was built. Some have been made into museums; others are still privately owned.

During most of the seventeenth century Sweden was at war. For a time the region's main industry was the manufacture of cannons. In 1862 a railroad was built connecting Södermanland with Göteborg, a major port city on the west coast. Since then industries have expanded and the countryside has become increasingly urban. As agriculture has declined, fields once used for crops or grazing stock have been planted with trees, mainly deciduous. Today these woodlands are inhabited by deer and many other kinds of wildlife.

Traditional dishes for Södermanland include *korngryn med fläsk* (barley pudding with pork) and *potatispudding* (potato pudding).

The following three recipes have been translated from Sörmländska Matminnen, *a book from Sörmland's museum in Nyköping featuring traditional recipes of the region.*

Barley Porridge and Pork *(Korngryn med fläsk)*

2 cups water
3/4 cup barley
1-1/3 cups milk
1 teaspoon salt
1 tablespoon dark corn syrup
1 teaspoon marjoram
brown sugar

Bring the water to a boil and add the barley. Simmer until the water is absorbed, about 30 minutes. Stir in the milk and season with salt, syrup, and marjoram. Cook slowly, uncovered, over low heat about 40 minutes, stirring occasionally. Sprinkle with brown sugar. Serve with fried pork and sautéed onion.

Potato Pudding with Fried Pork Slices *(Potatispudding)*

Ingegerd Wachtmeister of the Sörmland museum told me we should definitely include potato pudding as an example of Sörmland fare.

3 pounds potatoes, peeled and boiled
3/4 cup milk
1/3 cup flour
1 egg
3 tablespoons dark corn syrup
1 teaspoon salt
1/2 teaspoon pepper
2 to 3 teaspoons cinnamon
pork slices
lingonberries (optional, for topping)

Mash the potatoes. Mix in the milk, flour, and egg. Season with syrup, salt, pepper, and cinnamon.

Place the batter, which will be fairly heavy, in a greased, two-quart baking dish. Bake at 400° for about 1 hour. Allow the pudding to cool.

Fry pork slices in a pan. Pour off excess grease and then fry slices of the potato pudding in the same pan. Serve the fried pork and pudding slices together. Lingonberries make a nice topping.

Potato Pudding II

5 large carrots
10 medium-sized potatoes, skins on
3 eggs
1 cup light cream or milk
1-1/4 cups flour
1/4 cup dark corn syrup
2 teaspoons salt
black and/or white pepper to taste
butter or margarine

Cook the carrots and potatoes in lightly salted water, then peel and mash them together. Mix in the eggs, cream, and flour. Season with syrup, salt, and pepper. Pour into a well-greased baking dish (nonstick if possible). Dot with butter. Bake uncovered at 400° for about an hour. Loosen around edges; turn out onto a platter. After cooling, slice the pudding and fry. It's traditionally served with pork fried in the same pan.

Runestone (Runsten) *near Stockholm*

NÄRKE

"What kind of long crabs are those that creep over the fields?" asked the boy after a bit. "Plows and oxen. Plows and oxen," answered the wild geese.

—From *The Wonderful Adventures of Nils*
by Selma Lagerlöf

The tiny central province of Närke is bordered all around by five other provinces and enjoys easy access to three large lakes: Vänern, Vättern, and Hjälmaren.

The area has never been suitable for raising crops as only grass and hay grow well. Many early farmers made their living raising cattle. In the 1800s an overabundance of oxen led to the development of a shoe-making industry in the area. Today the largest industries, here as in many other provinces, are forestry, mining, and tourism.

Outdoor enthusiasts enjoy cross-country skiing in the winter and swimming at the white sand beach of Tiveden Park in the summer. Bird watching is a popular pastime at Lake Kvismaren and the nature reserve of Dovrasjödalen.

Örebro, Närke's largest city, is one of the oldest cities in the country. Its beautiful castle was originally built in the thirteenth century and then rebuilt in Renaissance style in the late 1500s. A summer festival is held here each year, with medieval-style entertainment and activities of all kinds including jousting tournaments. And what's a festival without food? Some local favorites include *abborre* (perch) from Lake Hjälmaren, *vitkålsoppa* (cabbage soup), *kåldolmar* (stuffed cabbage), and *äppelknyten* (baked apple).

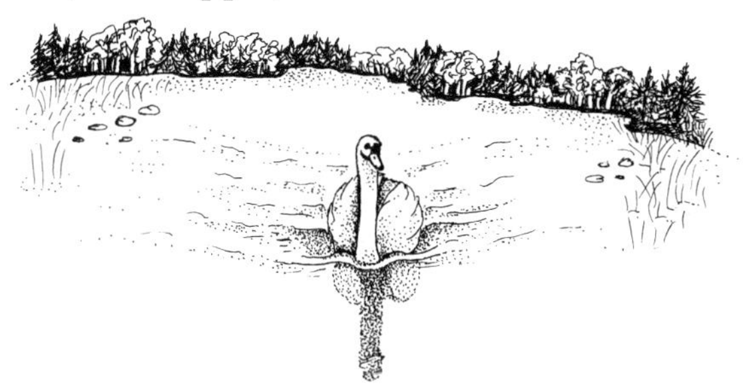

Oven-baked Perch *(Ugnsstekt abborre)*

8 small perch
6 tablespoons butter or margarine, divided
2 tablespoons fine bread crumbs
salt
white pepper
6 tablespoons chopped parsley, divided

Clean and rinse the fish well, then dry with a paper towel. Melt 4 tablespoons of the butter. Mix the bread crumbs with salt, pepper, and 2 tablespoons chopped parsley. Brush the fish with melted butter and dip in the bread crumb mixture to coat.

Place the fish, backs up, in a greased baking dish. Melt the remaining butter, mix in the remaining parsley, and pour over the fish. Bake in a very hot oven, 475°, until fish is nicely browned and flakes easily, about 20 minutes. Serves 4.

Örebro Castle

White Cabbage Soup with Meatballs
(Vitkålsoppa med frikadeller)

This recipe was contributed by Lennart Nilsson of Lekeberg Commune in Närke, who tells us that cabbage soup is a traditional favorite served each year at harvest time, especially on the first Tuesday of October.

Meatballs:
2 tablespoons dry bread crumbs
1/4 cup milk
1/2 pound ground meat
(70% beef, 30% pork)
1 teaspoon salt
dash of white pepper

Cabbage Soup:
1/2 large white cabbage head
(about 2 pounds)
butter or margarine
6 to 8 cups water
1 tablespoon salt
8 peppercorns
1 tablespoon corn syrup

Meatballs: Mix the bread crumbs into the milk and let stand for a few minutes. Mix well with the meat and spices. Form into small balls.

Soup: Remove the outer leaves and chop the cabbage into pieces. Sauté in butter in a frying pan, then transfer to a large pot. Add water and salt and bring to a boil. Add the peppercorns and syrup.

Simmer until the cabbage is almost cooked, about 20 minutes. Meanwhile, brown the meatballs in the frying pan. Add the meatballs to the soup. Simmer for 10 more minutes. Adjust seasonings. Serve with crispbread.

Stuffed Cabbage *(Kåldolmar)*

Kåldolmar, *(stuffed cabbage), originated in Turkey and was brought to Sweden about three hundred years ago by King Karl XII.*

1 head of cabbage
1 pound ground beef
2 green peppers, chopped fine
2 medium-sized onions, chopped fine
2 tablespoons vegetable oil
1 cup soft bread crumbs
1/3 cup chili sauce
2 teaspoons Worcestershire sauce
1/2 teaspoon salt
1/2 teaspoon marjoram
a few grains of pepper
1 (8-ounce) can tomato sauce
2 tablespoons butter or margarine
1/2 cup dairy sour cream

Core cabbage and cook, covered, 7 minutes in boiling, salted water. Remove twelve outer leaves. Cook ground beef, green peppers, and onions in oil until meat is browned. Add bread crumbs, chili sauce, Worcestershire sauce, and seasonings; mix well. Place equal amounts of meat mixture on each cabbage leaf. Roll and secure with wooden picks. (Start with stem end and fold edges in as you roll.) Place rolls in a large skillet. Pour tomato sauce over all. Dot with butter or margarine. Cover and simmer for about 1 hour. Remove cabbage rolls to a platter. Stir sour cream into tomato sauce in skillet and pour some of this mixture over the cabbage rolls. Serve remainder of sauce separately. Serves 6.

Note: This burns easily, so watch carefully. Cook remainder of head of cabbage until tender and save for another day to serve chopped and creamed in a cheese sauce.

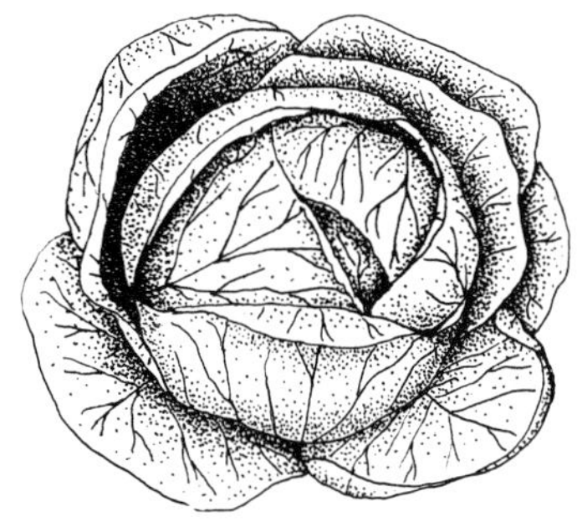

Baked Apples *(Äppelknyten)*

1-3/4 cups flour
1-1/4 cups cold butter, divided
4 or 5 tablespoons cold water
6 to 8 tart apples, peeled, cored
1/2 cup sugar mixed with
 1-1/2 teaspoons cinnamon
1/4 cup raisins (optional)
1 egg, beaten
1/4 cup almonds, chopped
 or ground

Cut flour into 1 cup butter; add water gradually and work into a dough. Refrigerate 30 minutes. Roll out on floured board, fold, and then chill again.

Preheat oven to 425°. Roll out the dough and cut into squares. The squares should be approximately 5 x 5" to 7 x 7", depending on the size of the apples.

Place an apple in the middle of each square. Fill apples with raisins and cinnamon-sugar, reserving a little of the sugar. Dot tops with remaining butter. Bring corners of pastry up over apples, pinching edges together. (The edges will seal better if moistened with a little water.) Brush with egg; sprinkle with cinnamon-sugar and almonds.

Bake for 5 minutes at 425°, then reduce heat to 325° and continue to bake another 45 to 50 minutes. Serve warm with vanilla sauce or ice cream.

Vanilla Sauce *(Vaniljsås)*

3 egg yolks, beaten
2 tablespoons sugar
1 cup cream
2 teaspoons vanilla extract
1 cup whipped cream

Mix egg yolks and sugar in top of double boiler. Add cream and cook until thick, stirring constantly. Remove from heat; add vanilla and cool, stirring occasionally. When completely cooled, fold in whipped cream.

DALSLAND

The valleys snuggled, light and smiling, between the dark mountains until they were gradually squeezed together by the hills.

—From *The Further Adventures of Nils Holgersson*
by Selma Lagerlöf

In Swedish, *dal* means valley, and there are certainly plenty of those in Dalsland. Rivers tumble down through the valleys from the deep, dark forests on the west toward Lake Vänern on the east. Small farm fields lie scattered here and there in the midst of the forest.

Despite the fertile land, farmers here suffered greatly during the famine years of the mid-1800s, and the area lost about sixty-four thousand of its inhabitants to emigration. Around 1870 the railroad went through, and soon after that the Dalsland Canal was built, both of which made transportation easier and encouraged the growth of industries such as paper mills and motor factories.

On the west, ties with neighboring Norway are obvious in the regional dialect. On the east, the shoreline of Lake Vänern with its archipelago makes a perfect place for fishing and sailing.

Some Dalsland farmers today grow and sell organic crops, including potatoes. Pork and potatoes are frequently found on the dinner table.

Hogs

Pork with Prunes *(Fläskfilé med katrinplommon)*

1 cup pitted prunes*
3 pounds lean pork loin
2 tablespoons lemon juice
1 teaspoon salt
1/4 teaspoon pepper
1 tablespoon butter or margarine for browning
1 cup bouillon for basting

Simmer the prunes in a little water until soft, then drain. Save the water for basting. Slit open the pork loin and insert the prunes. Bind or fasten shut with heavy toothpicks. Brush with lemon juice and sprinkle with salt and pepper. Brown the meat in butter and place in a roasting pan. Baste with the bouillon and a little of the prune water. Cover. Roast at 325° for 1-1/2 to 2 hours or until a meat thermometer inserted in thickest part reaches 160°. Baste as needed during roasting. Serves 6 to 8.

*In America, prunes are now often referred to as "dried plums."

Breaded Potato Bites *(Brynt potatis)*

6 to 8 medium-sized potatoes, peeled, boiled
2 tablespoons butter or margarine, divided
1 cup bread crumbs, divided
1 teaspoon salt, divided
1 teaspoon sugar, divided

Cut potatoes into 1/2-inch cubes. Brown 1 tablespoon butter in a skillet with 1/2 cup bread crumbs. Add half the potatoes, then salt and sugar. Stir continuously until the potatoes are coated with bread crumbs and well browned. Remove from pan and repeat with the remaining ingredients. Serves 6 to 8.

Potato Balls *(Potatisbullar)*

5 medium-sized potatoes
1 tablespoon melted butter
  or margarine
1 teaspoon sugar
1 teaspoon salt
1 egg, slightly beaten
3 tablespoons flour
1/2 cup fine dry bread crumbs
1/4 cup butter or margarine
  for frying

Cook and rice the potatoes. (Do not over cook; if the potatoes are water-logged it will be hard to form them into balls.) Add the melted butter, sugar, salt, egg, and flour. Mix thoroughly. Shape into small balls; should make about eighteen. Roll in bread crumbs to coat. Fry in butter or margarine, turning occasionally, until golden brown all around. Serves 6.

Bohuslän

BOHUSLÄN

As the boy gazed at the broad, endless sea and the red evening sun ... he felt a sense of peace and calm penetrate his soul.

—From *The Further Adventures of Nils Holgersson*
by Selma Lagerlöf

When one thinks of Bohuslän one thinks of the North Sea and of its rocky, barren archipelago. While the province does have fields and meadows, as well as deep forests, the seashore is its dominant feature, and fishing has always been its major occupation.

Back in the Stone Age, the province was covered by much more water than it is today. Since then the land has risen over 100 meters. The great shell banks of Uddevalla, located far inland, bear witness to the many forms of sea life that once existed here.

In Viking times the narrow strip of land that is Bohuslän belonged to Denmark. In the twelfth century Norway took possession. Over the years 1329–1523 there was a union between the Swedes, Danes, and Norwegians (the "Three Crowns"). In 1523 Gustav Vasa led a revolt that resulted in Sweden's independence. Denmark retained control of Norway, and Bohuslän was divided. War continued to rage in the area, on and off, for the next hundred years.

Finally, in 1658, Bohuslän officially became a part of Sweden, although most of its inhabitants didn't begin to speak Swedish until 1842 when nationwide compulsory education was established.

Prosperity in the region has risen and fallen with the supply of herring. For a time in the late 1800s, stone quarrying became profitable, and at the same time a number of health resorts were built along the oceanfront to cater to the rich and famous, beginning the tourism industry that is so important today. Fish and seafood of all kinds are popular regional fare.

Baked Cod *(Ungsbakad torsk)*

2 pounds of cod fillets
salt
white pepper
3 tablespoons lemon juice
1/2 cup sliced mushrooms
2 tablespoons butter or margarine
1 tablespoon flour
3/4 cup cream or milk
2 tomatoes, peeled and sliced thin
1/4 cup bread crumbs

Rinse the fillets, dry with a paper towel, and season with salt and pepper. Place in a shallow dish; add lemon juice and marinate several hours. Sauté the mushrooms in lightly browned butter. Add the flour and stir well. Gradually add the cream, stirring constantly. Simmer a few minutes, until sauce thickens. Season with salt and pepper.

Lay the fillets in a baking dish. Arrange the tomato slices on top; pour mushroom sauce over all. Sprinkle with bread crumbs. Bake uncovered in a hot oven (450°) about 15 to 20 minutes or until the fish is cooked through and golden brown. Serves 4.

Broiled Salmon with Dill Sauce *(Grillad lax med dillsås)*

salt and pepper
2 pounds salmon fillets
Sauce:*
1/2 cup mayonnaise
3 tablespoons lemon juice
2 tablespoons melted butter or margarine
1 teaspoon dill weed
1/2 teaspoon garlic powder
1/2 teaspoon lemon herb spice

Lightly salt and pepper the salmon, then broil, turning once, 2 to 3 minutes per side. Meat should be pink, not red, but do not over cook. Combine sauce ingredients and serve on the side. Serves 6.

*For best results, mix sauce ingredients the day before.

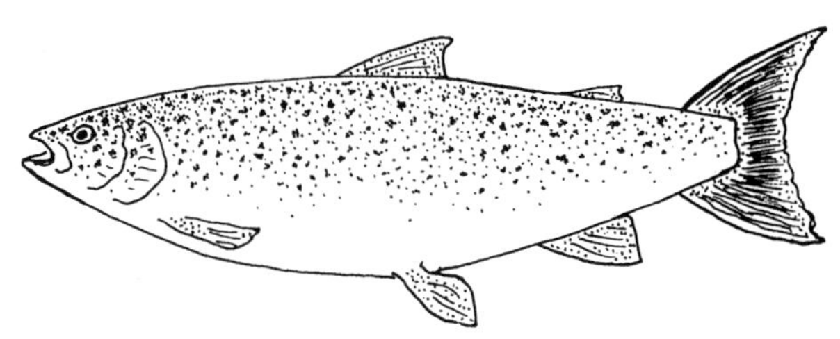

VÄSTERGÖTLAND

"How wonderful it all looks from up here!" he marveled. ... "It is a great country that we have! Wherever I go, there is always something new."

—From *The Further Adventures of Nils Holgersson*
by Selma Lagerlöf

Västergötland is a large province situated between Sweden's two largest lakes, Vänern and Vättern. To the south and east are dense forests of pine, fir, maple, oak, elm, and ash, but more than half the province is covered by a broad and fertile plain. Its far western point stretches out between Bohuslän to the north and Halland to the south, and touches the North Sea, where Göteborg, Sweden's second-largest city, lies.

In the 1800s when famine brought about mass emigration, many travelers first made their way to Göteborg, from there setting sail for the "new land." The port of Göteborg remains the largest in Scandinavia, and today there is also an international airport.

The Göta Canal

The 118-mile-long Göta Canal, shown previous page, opened in 1832, making it possible to travel across Sweden between Göteborg on the west coast and Motala on the east entirely by water. It's faster, however, to take the train. A leisurely cruise on the canal is more often enjoyed by tourists and vacationers.

Agriculture is still very important in the province, with a larger percentage of the population engaged in farming than the national average. Crops include oats, wheat, and barley. Beef cattle are raised, and there are two large slaughterhouses located at Skara and Skövde. Dairy farms have made the province well known for its production of cheese.

In modern times industry and manufacturing have increased in importance. Volvo automobiles are manufactured in Göteborg, while some of the country's largest mail-order companies are located in the Borås region. Other industries include a large hydroelectric power plant at Trollhätten and an Electrolux factory.

Tourism, here as elsewhere, is encouraged. Visitors to Västergötland may see archeological finds dating back to the Stone Age, including *gånggrifter*, stone-lined passageways that lead into burial chambers, and *hällkistor*, the chambers themselves. Treasure chests of beautiful gold jewelry from AD 400 to 500 and many other items are displayed in museums. Church historians will be interested to learn that Västergötland was the first Swedish province to adopt Christianity and was the seat of the first Swedish bishop, at Skara, in the tenth century.

Many fairs and festivals are held in Västergötland every summer. The town of Alingås hosts a potato festival in June, and Skara puts on a pancake festival each July.

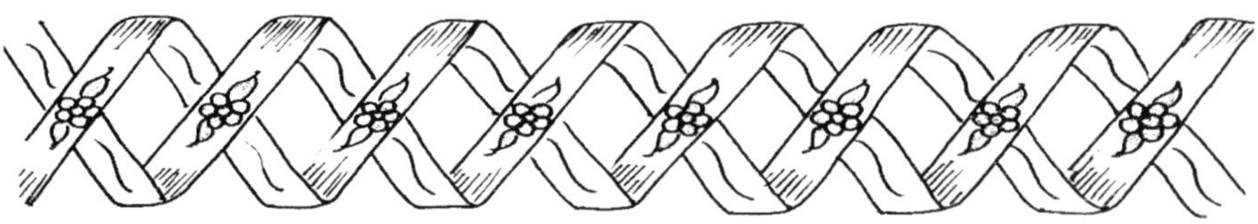

Potato Pancakes *(Raggmunkar)*

This recipe was contributed by Barbro Halvorsson, who lives in Västergötland. Barbro and I became friends through the Internet. We correspond regularly by e-mail, and Barbro has helped me immensely with research for this book.

3/4 cup flour
2 teaspoons salt
1-3/4 cups milk, divided
1 egg
8 large white potatoes
bacon grease (or butter or margarine) for frying

Mix the flour and salt and blend with a little of the milk to a smooth, lump-free consistency. Add the rest of the milk and the egg. Mix well. Peel and grate the potatoes. Cover with boiling water and let stand for 2 minutes, then drain well. Stir the potatoes into the batter.

Heat the grease in a frying pan or griddle. Spoon on the batter and fry as thin pancakes. Serve with lingonberry jam and meat, traditionally pork. Serves 6.

Note: You can also precook the potatoes, then drain and rice or mash them.

Fig Pudding *(Fikonpudding)*

10 ounces figs
4 eggs, separated
3/4 cup sugar
1 cup cream
1 tablespoon dried bread crumbs
3/4 cup chopped sweet almonds

In the baking dish:
2 teaspoons butter or margarine
3 tablespoons bread crumbs

Cut the figs into strips, place in a saucepan, cover with water, and simmer until swollen, then drain. Blend the egg yolks with the sugar, figs, cream, and bread crumbs. Beat the egg whites until stiff; fold into the fig mixture, along with the almonds.

Butter a baking dish and sprinkle with bread crumbs. Pour the pudding mix in. Bake at 350° for 30 to 40 minutes. Turn upside down onto a serving platter. Serve with vanilla sauce. (See recipe, page 51.) Serves 6.

ÖSTERGÖTLAND

"There can't be any peasants in this land," he said to himself, "since I do not see any peasant farms." Immediately all the wild geese shrieked, "Here the peasants live like gentlemen. Here the peasants live like gentlemen."

—From *The Wonderful Adventures of Nils*
by Selma Lagerlöf

Östergötland lies to the east, between Lake Vättern and the Baltic Sea. The center of this province is covered by a flat and fertile agricultural plain, while to the north and south there are wooded hills, pine and fir in the highlands, broad-leaf trees in the east, oak and lime trees *(lind)* along the coastline.

Östergötland is blessed with a rich history. Rock carvings near the city of Norrköping whisper secrets of ancient beginnings, and runestones tell of Viking times. The most famous of these is Rökstenen, which dates back to AD 800.

During the ninth century Östergötland was converted to Christianity and Linköping became an Episcopal city. In 1132 Sverker Eriksson, a nobleman of a tribe of Östergötland magnates, married the widow of the last Stenkil king and was acknowledged king of Sweden. The important position held by the province during his reign contributed to its growth in trade and industry.

One local noblewoman became one of Sweden's most celebrated personalities. Birgitta Birgersdotter experienced more than six hundred visions, which were written down and widely read in the late Middle Ages. She was involved in European and Swedish politics and made many pilgrimages. In 1391 she was canonized by the Church in Rome. In 1999 Pope John Paul II named her one of the six patron saints of Europe. In 2003 the seven hundred-year anniversary of her birth was celebrated in Vadstena, site of a convent that houses her relics.

Over the years, iron ore mining, copper and brass production, and a textile industry have become important. Today Linköping is a modern industrial city with a SAAB Aircraft factory and a thriving computer industry, reflecting the city's focus on science and technology. It is also the home of Linköping University, which has a second campus in Norrköping.

Visitors to Östergötland may enjoy seeing many historical sites or bird watching at Lake Tåkern, one of Northern Europe's finest bird lakes. A visit will surely involve water in some way—perhaps a cruise along the Göta Canal, or fishing in one of the many lakes and streams or along the east coast archipelago.

A favorite vegetable here in Östergötland is kohlrabi.

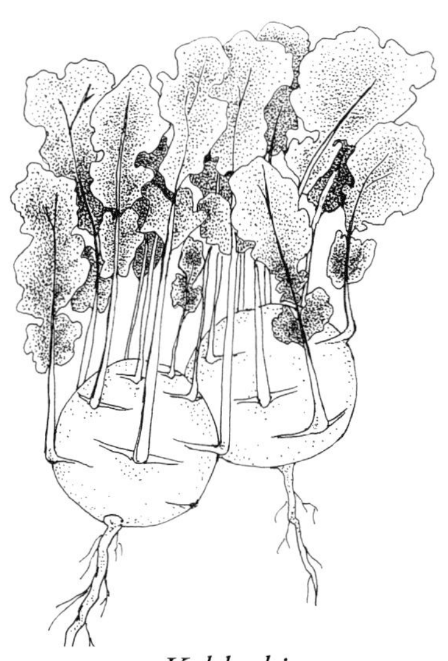

Kohlrabi

Pork Fillet with Kohlrabi and Mushrooms
(Fläskfilé med kålrabbi och kantareller)

2 cups diced kohlrabi
water
2 tablespoons vinegar
1 tablespoon butter or margarine
1-1/2 pounds pork fillets
(or boneless chops)
salt and pepper
1 cup water or bouillon
1/2 teaspoon salt
1 to 2 cups chantarelle or other
mushrooms
1 tablespoon flour
1/2 cup water

Peel and dice the kohlrabi into half-inch cubes. Cover with water and vinegar. Let stand for 1 hour. Melt the butter in a frying pan. Brown the meat; season with salt and pepper. Add bouillon and simmer, covered, for about an hour, until cooked through. Drain the kohlrabi; rinse and place in a saucepan. Cover with fresh water and add salt. Simmer for 20 to 30 minutes. Drain.

In a separate frying pan, sauté the mushrooms and brown the kohlrabi.

Remove the pork to a serving platter and keep warm. Mix the flour with 1/2 cup water and stir this into the pan drippings. Simmer for a couple minutes.

Pour half the gravy over the pork. Stir the kohlrabi and mushrooms into the remaining gravy, then serve on the platter alongside the meat.

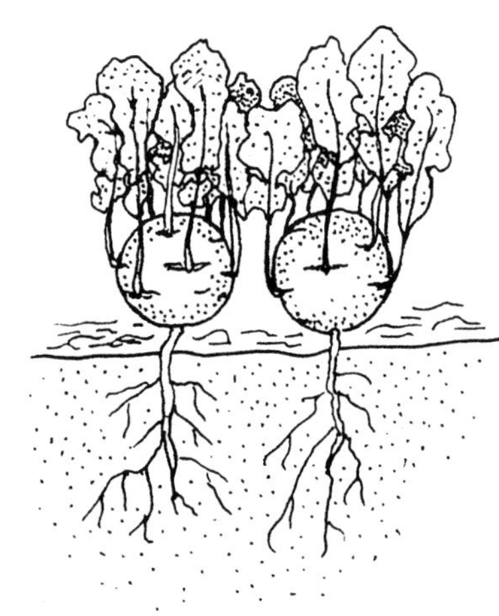

Kohlrabi in the ground

Kohlrabi with Egg *(Kålrabbi med ägg)*

2 cups diced kohlrabi
4 cups water, divided
2 tablespoons vinegar
1/2 teaspoon salt
2 tablespoons butter
2 tablespoons flour
1 cup milk
1/4 teaspoon salt
1/8 teaspoon pepper
1 hard-cooked egg, diced

Peel and dice the kohlrabi. Mix 2 cups water with vinegar and pour over the kohlrabi. Soak for 1 hour. Drain and rinse. Cover with 2 cups fresh water, add 1/2 teaspoon salt, and simmer for 20 to 30 minutes. Drain; set aside. In a small saucepan, melt the butter and blend in the flour. Add milk gradually, stirring constantly. Reduce heat and cook about 3 minutes. Add the salt and pepper and gently stir in the diced egg. Pour sauce over the kohlrabi.

Blueberry Parfait *(Blåbärsparfait)*

Fresh blueberries are best, especially if you have gathered them from the forest yourself!

2/3 cup sugar, divided
1/2 cup water
3 egg yolks, well beaten
1 teaspoon vanilla extract
2-1/2 cups blueberries plus more for topping
1-1/2 cups whipping cream

Mix 1/3 cup sugar into the water and bring to a boil. Remove from heat. Mix the egg yolks into the hot sugar water, stirring constantly. Return to heat and gently simmer for 2 to 3 minutes, stirring constantly. When thickened, pour into a bowl and allow to cool while continuing to stir. Add the vanilla. Mix the blueberries with the remaining 1/3 cup sugar, then add this to the previous mixture.

Whip the cream until stiff. Gently fold into the blueberry mixture. Pour into individual serving dishes and freeze. Remove from freezer about 1/2 hour before serving. Serve topped with a dab of whipped cream and one large or several small whole blueberries.

SOUTHERN PROVINCES

SMÅLAND

And so our Lord created the Smålander, and made him quick-witted and contented and happy and thrifty and enterprising and capable to get his livelihood in his poor country.

—From *The Wonderful Adventures of Nils*
by Selma Lagerlöf

It is said of Smålanders that they are especially hardy and industrious, that they must be in order to wrest a living from the poor and stony soil of their province. And while it is true that agriculture here has always been a struggle, Småland is rich in beauty and in many other ways as well.

Writers have found it a rich source of material. Wilhelm Moberg, author of *The Emigrants* series, was inspired by the lives of its common folk during the mid-1800s. Astrid Lindgren, creator of Pippi Longstocking, was born and raised here, as was the winner of the 1951 Nobel Prize for Literature, Pär Lagerkvist.

Scientist Carl von Linné began his pioneering work on plant classification in Småland, and the regional flower Linnaea Borealis is named for him. Other famous natives include singer Jenny Lind and contemporary tennis stars Mats Wilander and Stefan Edberg.

The forests of Småland are a national treasure, for recreation as well as for the timber industry. Deer and moose are found in large numbers, especially because there are no longer any wolves. There are also grouse, rabbits, fox, badgers, a few martens, and plenty of fish in the streams and lakes.

Swedish crystal is world renowned, and Småland is home to the "kingdom of glass," with seventeen of Sweden's best-known glassworks concentrated in the radius of a few miles. Here visitors can watch master craftsmen at work, blowing, shaping, and engraving crystal.

Småland is also rich in history, and no visit to the province would be complete without seeing Kalmar Castle, a magnificent fortress on the east coast surrounded by thick stone walls and a moat with a drawbridge. The Emigrant Museum at Växjö is very interesting, especially to anyone with Swedish ancestors, as it tells the story of their lives before they left Sweden, their journey, and some of the hardships they encountered upon reaching their destination.

The people of Småland are warm and hospitable, and very good cooks. Many of their traditional recipes have to do with making the most out of little, but today's cook knows how to put on a feast! One must be sure to sample some of their traditional *köttbullar* (meatballs), *rågbröd* (rye bread), and *ostkaka* (cheesecake).

Swedish Meatballs *(Köttbullar)*

I remember our first morning in Småland, in 1991. We had stayed the night at the home of Erik Johansson, my father's cousin. As we came downstairs we smelled something delicious cooking. The table was already set with an amazing variety of eggs, pickles, cheeses, breads, butter, and preserves, as well as honey from the hives Erik's son Inge keeps. Best of all, there was Margit at the stove, frying meatballs. What a breakfast!

1/2 cup milk
2 eggs
1 cup bread crumbs
2 tablespoons butter or margarine
1 to 2 medium-sized onions, diced
1 pound lean ground beef
1/2 pound ground veal
1/2 pound ground pork
1 teaspoon salt
1/2 teaspoon pepper
1/2 teaspoon allspice

Mix the milk and eggs together in a large bowl, add the bread crumbs, and allow to stand for a few minutes. Melt the butter in a frying pan. Sauté the onion until tender. Add the meat, onion, and seasonings to the egg mixture and mix it all together with a fork, lightly. Form the meat into small, round balls with wet hands. Fry the meatballs a few at a time over medium heat until they are cooked through, turning frequently to keep them round. Serves 4 to 6.

Rye Bread *(Rågbröd)*

This is the rye bread recipe used by my grandmother Anna Elge. She never measured anything, so one day I followed her around the kitchen, stopping her to measure things as she went along. Since then I have used this recipe myself many times, and always feel as if my grandmother is with me.

2 packages yeast
2 teaspoons white sugar
2/3 cup lukewarm water
1-1/3 cups milk
1/4 cup margarine
2 to 3 tablespoons dark molasses
1/3 cup brown sugar
1-1/2 teaspoons salt
about 4 cups white flour, divided
1-1/3 cups rye flour
melted butter or margarine

Dissolve the yeast and white sugar in the water. Heat the milk until it is almost, but not quite, boiling. Add the margarine, molasses, brown sugar, and salt and stir well. Pour into a large mixing bowl and allow to cool until lukewarm or tepid. Stir in the yeast mixture and about 2 cups of white flour. Mix very well. Let this rise until doubled (about 45 minutes).

Add the rye flour and the rest of the white flour. Mix with a large spoon, then turn out onto a breadboard and knead with your hands. Add more flour as needed.

Shape into two loaves and place in loaf pans. Prick the tops with a fork, cover with a cloth, and allow to rise again for about an hour in a warm place. Preheat the oven to 350°.

Before baking, brush the tops with melted butter or margarine. Bake for about 50 to 60 minutes. (Time will vary depending on individual oven temperature.) As soon as you remove the loaves from the oven, brush the tops again with butter or margarine.

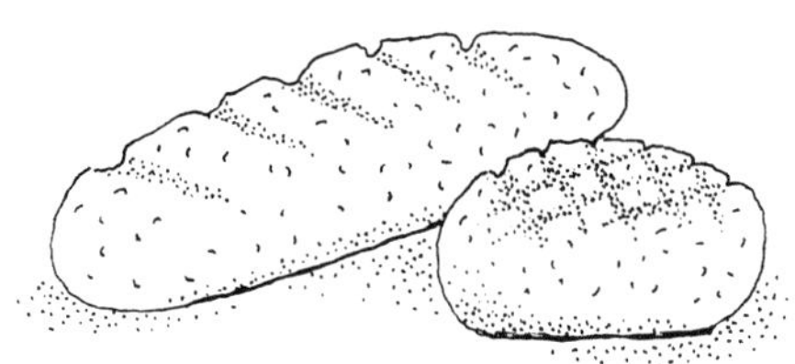

Cheesecake *(Ostkaka)*

Swedish cheesecake is kind of a cross between custard and cottage cheese. Here's the old-fashioned method for making it, still practiced by some of the women here in Stanton.

1 gallon raw whole milk
1/4 rennet tablet, crushed
(use cheese rennet, not the type for making ice cream)
2 tablespoons warm water
1/2 cup flour
1 teaspoon salt
3 eggs
3/4 cup sugar
1 teaspoon vanilla

Allow the milk to stand unrefrigerated overnight. In the morning, set aside 1-1/2 cups milk. Heat the rest of the milk to lukewarm, about 100°. Dissolve the rennet in the water.

Mix about 1 cup of the warm milk with the flour and salt; beat well until there are no lumps. Add this mixture to the rest of the warm milk, and also add the rennet. Heat and stir gently until it thickens and curdles. Remove from heat. Pour into a large square or rectangular pan.

Set aside for about 30 minutes. Cut through with a knife in diagonal lines (crisscross), both directions, making "diamonds" about 1-1/2 inches square. Let stand about 30 minutes to allow the whey to separate.

Pour the cheese mixture into a collander and allow to drain for at least 3 hours, turning occasionally, then crumble the mixture into a buttered 3-quart casserole.

Beat the eggs, sugar, reserved 1-1/2 cups milk, and vanilla together. Pour over the cheese and stir gently.

Bake at 300° for 1-1/2 to 2 hours until it is firm like custard and an inserted knife comes out clean. The top should be lightly browned. Serve with *kräm* (fruit sauce), page 69.

Ostkaka with Powdered Milk

Traditional ostkaka *recipes call for raw, unhomogenized milk, which may be hard to obtain. Attempts with homogenized milk are seldom successful. The following alternative recipe was contributed by Jeannie Peterson, who challenges anyone to tell the difference.*

1-2/3 cups powdered milk
5 cups warm water (about 101° to 105°)
1/3 cup flour
1 rennet tablet, crushed and dissolved in 1 tablespoon warm water (use cheese rennet; the type for custard or ice cream won't work)
2 eggs, beaten
1/3 cup sugar
1/2 teaspoon vanilla
1/2 cup condensed milk, undiluted

In a bowl, mix the powdered milk thoroughly with the warm water. Mix the flour with about 1/2 cup of this milk until it is smooth and has no lumps, then gradually add the rest of the milk and the dissolved rennet. Stir well.

Allow to set about 30 to 40 minutes, then cut through with a table knife in a crisscross pattern. Allow to stand undisturbed for another 40 minutes. (These times are approximate. It may take longer.)

With a ladle, gently remove whey as it forms at the surface and along the edges. When the mass is firm enough, you may transfer to a collander. Drain off a total of 16 to 18 ounces of whey and discard.

Mix the beaten eggs with the sugar, vanilla, and condensed milk. Stir all ingredients together and pour into an 8 x 8" pan that has been sprayed with nonstick spray.

Bake at 325° for about 1 hour, until a knife inserted in the center comes out clean. Cool completely. Serve with fruit sauce (next page) or berries. May be stored frozen.

Ostkaka with Cottage Cheese

A quick and easy way to make ostkaka *is to bypass the rennet and whey step, and start with cottage cheese. Traditionalists may shake their heads, but many find the end result acceptable.*

16 ounces small curd cottage cheese
2 tablespoons flour
3 eggs
1/3 cup sugar
1/2 teaspoon vanilla
1 cup cream

Press the cottage cheese through a sieve. Stir in the flour. Beat the eggs; add the sugar, vanilla, and cream. Blend well with the cottage cheese mixture. Pour into a greased 8 x 8" inch baking pan. Bake at 350° for 1 to 1-1/4 hours.

Fruit Sauce *(Kräm)*

2-1/2 cups grape juice (or any other fruit juice)
1/4 teaspoon salt
1 tablespoon lemon juice
1/2 cup sugar
1/2 cup cornstarch

Mix all ingredients together and cook in a double boiler until the mixture thickens. Serve warm or cold.

Kalmar Castle

HALLAND

Here again was a place where land and sea met, in such a pretty and peaceful sort of way, just as if they tried to show each other the best and loveliest which they possessed.

—From *The Wonderful Adventures of Nils*
by Selma Lagerlöf

In medieval times Sweden's three southernmost provinces belonged to Denmark. After the death of King Waldemar II in 1241, the Swedes pushed across Halland to the western sea, built Älvborg's castle, and created the border that exists today. Nevertheless, over the next few centuries the position of Halland and parts thereof changed several times, becoming Danish, Swedish, or Norwegian as a result of various marriages and alliances. Finally, following a Danish defeat in the war of 1643–1645, a treaty was signed making Halland Swedish, and so it has remained ever since.

A wide, white sandy beach extends along most of the western coastline, which becomes rougher and more rocky at its northern end. Inland from the shore lies a fertile plain that gradually changes over to forest as it nears the eastern border with Småland and Västergötland. Four large rivers run westward through the province on their way to the sea. Where once their rapids turned millstones to grind grain, today they create hydroelectric power.

Fishing and farming are equally important here. Some favorite regional recipes are *fisksoppa* (fish soup), *Varbergsbröd* (Varberg's biscuits), and *kanelbullar* (cinnamon rolls).

The following two recipes were contributed by Jean Detloff, great-granddaughter of Rev. Bengt Magnus Halland, the founder of my hometown of Stanton, Iowa. Jean got them when visiting in Halland.

Fish Soup *(Fisksoppa)*

2 large carrots, peeled and grated
1 leek, thinly sliced, white and green
1 (16-ounce) can tomato sauce
5 cups water
2 vegetable bouillon cubes
2 teaspoons fennel seeds
1 bunch fresh dill
1/2 pound cod fillet (or other mild whitefish)
1/2 pound small shrimp
1 cup cream or milk

Combine carrots, leek, tomato sauce, and water and bring to a boil. Add vegetable bouillon cubes and cook for a few minutes. Put the fennel seeds in a tea strainer and "dangle" in the soup for most of the cooking time. Keep tasting so that the fennel taste doesn't become too strong. Snip the dill into the soup. Set aside. (You may cool the soup at this time and finish it later.) Flake the cod, add it and the shrimp to the soup, and heat. Simmer for a short time. Add the cream and heat, but do not boil. Serve with bread and cheese. Serves 6.

Varberg Biscuits *(Varbergsbröd)*

Are these biscuits, or are they cookies? Either way, they are delicious!

1/2 pound powdered sugar
2 eggs
1-3/4 cups white flour
1/2 teaspoon baking powder
1 egg, beaten, for glazing
slivered almonds

Preheat oven to 400°. Mix the sugar and eggs together well. Stir in the flour and baking powder. Allow dough to rise 15 minutes, then turn onto a floured breadboard and roll out thin (about 3/4 inch). Cut out the biscuits. (If you use a 2-1/4-inch diameter cutter, you should get two dozen.) Brush the tops with the beaten egg. Sprinkle the almonds on top. Place the biscuits on a lightly greased cookie sheet and bake about 10 minutes.

Cinnamon Rolls *(Kanelbullar)*

This was contributed by Ingrid Kampås, who lives in Ullared in the province of Halland. Ingrid is a nurse, a writer, and famous, at least in her own family, she says, for her bread baking.

3 tablespoons butter or margarine
2 cups milk
2 packets dry yeast
1 egg
1 tablespoon ground cardamom seed
1/3 cup sugar
1 teaspoon salt
flour (4-1/2 to 5 cups)

For Filling and Topping:
butter or margarine
cinnamon
sugar
1 egg, beaten (optional)
pearl sugar or nuts (optional)
powdered sugar plus milk (optional)

Melt the butter, add the milk, and heat to lukewarm. Dissolve the yeast in a little of the liquid, then add the rest. Mix in the egg, cardamom, sugar, and salt. Add the flour gradually. Use an electric mixer at first until the dough becomes too thick, then a wooden spoon and, finally, turn the dough out onto a floured board and knead gently. Return to the bowl and cover with a cloth. Allow to rise 45 minutes in a warm place. Turn the dough out onto the board and roll it out until it is about 12 x 18" and about 1/2 inch thick.

Spread a layer of butter on the dough, then sprinkle cinnamon and sugar generously on it. Roll into a roll from the long side (so that the roll will be about 18 inches long). Cut into 1-inch slices. Lay the slices on a lightly greased baking sheet, cover, and allow to rise 30 minutes. Bake at 375° until rolls are golden brown, about 10 minutes or so.

Option 1: Prior to baking, brush the tops with beaten egg and sprinkle with pearl sugar or nuts.

Option 2: After baking, mix powdered sugar with a little milk and drizzle over the tops while still warm.

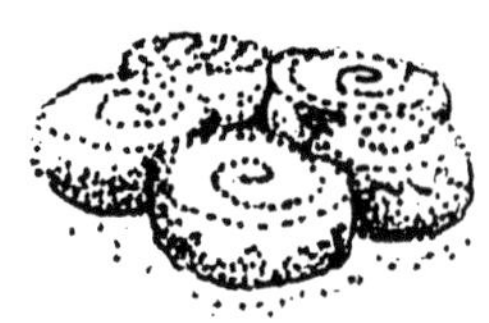

BLEKINGE

And since he could not sleep, he sat there and saw how pretty it looked when sea and land meet, here in Blekinge.

—From *The Wonderful Adventures of Nils*
by Selma Lagerlöf

Blekinge is the smallest mainland province. Many Vikings once lived in this area. One of the oldest runestones in Sweden is Blekinge's Björketorp Sten, which dates back to AD 600.

One usually thinks of the Vikings as warriors, sailing the high seas, discovering new territories, fighting and pillaging. But these warriors also had wives, children, and homes where they lived when they were not at sea. In Blekinge the fertile soil provided good pasture for their cattle and easy access for their ships to come and go along the coastline.

The Blekinge Vikings traded mostly with the islands of Öland and Gotland, and with the "Swedes" in Birka on Lake Mälaren. Occasionally, however, they made longer journeys. Sometimes ships went down, and treasures were later found on the ocean bottom. One of the most famous is the *Johannisskatten*. It contained 2,400 coins from Arabic countries, Byzantine, Germany, and England.

During the fifteenth and sixteenth centuries, Blekinge traded hands between Denmark and Sweden several times. Wars during the seventeenth century resulted in numerous castles and forts being built across the countryside, some of which still stand. In 1658 Blekinge became Swedish and has since remained so.

Karlskrona is the capital and a major port city. During the mass emigration years of the nineteenth century, many Swedes left from Karlshamn (Karl's Harbor). Today a statue that stands there commemorates that mass exodus. The northern part of Blekinge is covered with forests, while the south is a flat, coastal landscape. The trees are mostly oak, birch, and beech. Hawthorn grows around the meadows.

Despite the growth of industry, many of Blekinge's inhabitants still depend on fishing for their livelihoods. Fishing is popular with tourists, too, both in the sea and in the lakes and streams.

Salmon Stock Soup *(Laxryggsoppa)*

This recipe comes from Hälleviks Rökeri in western Blekinge and was provided by Susanne Ström. It calls for the use of fish bones after the fillets have been removed, which Susanne tells us was common in the past during hard times. One sold the best portion and kept what was left for one's own use. For a richer soup, bits of fillet meat may also be cut up and added.

1-1/2 pounds salmon (after fillets have been removed)
4 cups water with a few drops of vinegar
1-1/2 teaspoons salt (less if using salted fish)
fresh dill sprigs
1/2 yellow onion, sliced
1 to 2 bay leaves
4 peppercorns
4 potatoes
3 to 4 carrots
1 leek
1 cup frozen peas
cream or milk (optional)
flour (optional)

Boil the fish bones, with the attached meat, in the water together with vinegar, salt, and dill sprigs for 10 to 15 minutes. Remove the fish and set aside. Strain the stock; add the onion, bay leaves, and peppercorns. Return to a simmer. Peel the potatoes and carrots and cut them into pieces. Slice the leek. Add all the vegetables to the simmering stock. (Other vegetables, such as celery, may be used, according to season and personal preference.) Cooking time will vary depending upon how soft one likes the vegetables. The peas can be added shortly before the other ingredients are done.

Pick the remaining fish meat off the bones and either stir into the soup or serve on the side. Serve with a hearty bread and a glass of dark beer.

If a richer soup is desired, stir in milk or cream thickened with a bit of flour. In this case, crispbread and a glass of dry, white wine are recommended.

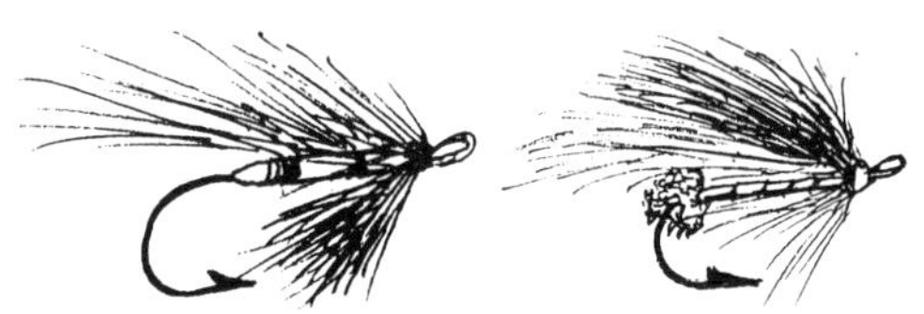

Fruit Soup *(Fruktsoppa)*

by Susanne Ström

2/3 cup dried pear slices
2/3 cup dried apple slices
5 cups water plus more to cover fruit
10 pitted prunes
1/2 cup raisins
1 cup red fruit juice (grape, raspberry, etc.)
3/4 cup sugar
3 tablespoons potato flour (may substitute cornstarch)

Place the pear and apple slices in a bowl. Add enough water to cover and allow to soak until soft. Drain. Place all the fruit in a saucepan; add 5 cups water, fruit juice, and sugar. Simmer 15 minutes. Stir the potato flour into the soup. (Potato flour won't dissolve in cold water like wheat flour will. Better to stir it directly into the simmering soup.) Simmer a few more minutes. Serve either warm or cold. It makes an excellent accompaniment to a fish entrée.

SKÅNE

"What kind of a big, checked cloth is this that I'm looking down on?" said the boy to himself without expecting anyone to answer him. But instantly, the wild geese who flew about him called out: "Fields and meadows. Fields and meadows."

—From *The Wonderful Adventures of Nils*
by Selma Lagerlöf

Skåne is the most "Danish" Swedish province. Before becoming a permanent part of Sweden in 1658, it belonged to Denmark for more than eight hundred years, and many Danish cultural influences remain. Skåne residents are proud of their somewhat unique status and their double heritage.

Once archenemies, the two countries fought long and hard for control of this rich province, as evidenced by the many fortresses and castles scattered across the landscape. On the other hand, stately homes and estates bear witness to a history of prosperity.

The province is large, with wide expanses of flat and fertile fields at its center, forested hills in the north, and a coastline on three sides. To the east lies the Baltic Sea and to the west the North Sea, where, at its nearest point, Denmark is only about 10 miles across the sound. In July 2000 both countries celebrated the opening of a bridge connecting the cities of Malmö, Sweden, and Copenhagen, Denmark. This bridge project, which includes an underground tunnel and an artificial island, is intended to facilitate travel and trade between the two countries.

Malmö, Skåne's capital and the country's third-largest city, is the heart of southern Sweden's financial district, with many insurance companies and financial institutions. But while the cities bustle with modern life, a peaceful, rural past lives on in the countryside, where farming still takes place.

Tourists come to Skåne for many reasons. Miles of shoreline beckon with sandy beaches for swimming, fishing, and boating.

The island of Ven, off the coast of Landskrona, permits no automobile traffic and is a popular destination for sailboat enthusiasts. Nature reserves and forests appeal to some, while others enjoy the lively entertainment of clubs and theater in the cities. The past can be revisited in places like the magnificent twelfth-century Lund Cathedral, with its medieval astronomical clock, or the ancient and mysterious Ale stones at Kåseberg, fifty-eight huge vertical stones placed in the shape of a 67-meter-long ship.

The people of Skåne love to eat, and insist that the food be good. A special feast is held each year on St. Mårten's Day, the eleventh of November. The legend of St. Mårtin tells of the time he was to be installed as bishop, an honor he did not desire. When his parishioners came looking for him he hid in a goose pen, but the geese cackled loudly and gave him away. In anger, the priest ordered the geese slaughtered, and to this day a goose feast is served each year on St. Mårten's Day.

Other regional specialties include all kinds of seafood, and when the natives entertain, they bring out their very best!

Skåne is noted for windmills.

Skåne Castle of Glimmingehus

The following three recipes come from Gunilla Wiberg, my cousin Paul's wife. They live in the city of Hässleholm, in Skåne. Paul and Gunilla, along with their daughter Sara, have visited us twice here in Stanton, and were most gracious hosts when we were in Sweden. Gunilla loves to cook, which is a good thing, because Paul loves to eat!

Roast Goose *(Stekt gås)*

1 young goose
1/2 lemon
1 tablespoon salt
white pepper
Stuffing *(Fyllning)*:
7 medium-sized apples, sliced
1/2 pound seedless prunes

Gravy *(Skysås)*:
1 tablespoon potato flour
salt and pepper
soy sauce
To Garnish:
plums
sprigs of parsley

Thaw the goose, if frozen, and remove giblets. Rinse and dry the bird and rub with lemon, inside and out. Season inside and out with salt and pepper, and fill the cavity with the apples and prunes. Bind up the bird and place it on a rack, breast up.

Roast in the oven on the lowest rack at 350°, without basting, 2-1/2 to 3 hours. Stick with a testing nail in the thickest part of the thigh. When the juice runs clear with no trace of pink the bird is done. (Using a meat thermometer stuck in the thickest part of the thigh, roast until the temperature reaches 185°.)

Drain off the drippings for gravy. Return the goose to the oven for about 10 minutes, so that the skin will become slightly crisp. If the skin has already become quite brown, cover the bird loosely with aluminum foil. During this time allow the oven door to remain slightly ajar.

Strain the drippings. Blend the flour with a little water and stir into the drippings, bringing it to a boil. Season to taste with salt, pepper, and soy.

Carve the goose and place the meat on a platter, garnishing with plums and sprigs of parsley. Serves 8 to 10.

Black Soup (also known as Blood Soup) *(Svartsoppa)*

neck of one goose
5 cups water
salt to taste
5 white peppercorns
4 whole cloves
1 yellow onion, sliced
1/2 pound seedless prunes
3-1/2 cups water, divided
1/3 cup sugar
1 pound apples, sliced

Soup ***(Soppa)*****:**
2 tablespoons butter or margarine
1/3 cup flour
4 cups bouillon
4 cups stock
1-1/2 cups goose or pig blood
1 teaspoon white pepper
1 teaspoon cloves
1 teaspoon ginger
3 tablespoons sugar
3 ounces vinegar
3 ounces cognac
6 ounces red wine
3 ounces fruit juice
goose liver sausage, sliced

Rinse the neck well. Place in a saucepan, cover with 5 cups water, and allow to slowly come to a boil. Skim froth and add salt, peppercorns, four cloves, and onion. Simmer about 2 hours. Strain, saving the stock to be used in the soup. Cool. Slice the neck into pieces and remove all bones.

Rinse the prunes and allow to stand in 1 cup water about 30 minutes, then drain and set aside. In a saucepan, mix 2-1/2 cups water with sugar to make a syrup. Cook the apples in syrup until they are soft. Drain and set aside.

Melt the butter and stir in the flour, then gradually add cold bouillon, stirring continuously. Add the stock and bring to a boil. Allow to simmer 10 minutes. Strain broth and return to the pan. Strain the blood and mix it into the soup, stirring briskly. Allow to simmer about 10 more minutes but be careful not to scorch; stir continuously. Season with salt, pepper, 1 teaspoon cloves, ginger, and sugar. Add vinegar, cognac, wine, and fruit juice. Adjust seasonings. To keep warm, a double boiler works best.

Place the neck meat, prunes, apples, and sliced goose liver as accompaniment on a platter and serve with the soup.

Filled Pancakes *(Bjudpannkakor/crêpes)*

Batter:
3 eggs
1/2 cup flour
1/2 teaspoon salt
1 cup milk
1/2 cup whipping cream

Filling: Dilled Shrimp
***(Fyllning: Dillstruvade Räkor)*:**
1-1/2 tablespoons butter
2-1/2 tablespoons flour
2/3 cup milk
1/2 cup whipping cream
4 ounces shrimp (shells removed)
3 tablespoons finely minced fresh dill
salt
pepper

Preheat the oven to 425°. In a mixing bowl, beat the eggs well; blend in the flour and salt. Add the milk gradually; mix to a smooth consistency. Add the cream.

Line the bottom of a 12 x 16" baking tray with baking-tray paper. Pour and spread the batter. Bake in the middle of the oven about 15 minutes. (The batter will "bubble up" quite a bit during this time.)

While the pancake is baking you can make the filling: Melt the butter in a saucepan; blend in the flour. Gradually add the milk and cream. (The consistency should be rather thick.) Simmer 3 to 5 minutes. Mix in the shrimp and dill. Season to taste with salt and pepper.

When the pancake is done, remove it from the oven, turn onto a sheet of aluminum foil, and immediately peel off the baking paper.

Spread the filling over the pancake. Roll together lengthwise. Transfer to a serving platter. Cut into portions, or you may invite guests to cut their own. Serve warm with a salad of mixed greens. Serves 4.

Note: Various types of filling may be used. With fruit, for example, it makes a nice dessert.

GOTLAND

Little children played ring games, and sang as they played. ... After that the boy could never think of Gotland without thinking of the games and songs at the same time.

—From *The Wonderful Adventures of Nils*
by Selma Lagerlöf

Two large islands lie off the east coast of the Swedish mainland. The largest is Gotland, about 109 miles long and 31 miles wide, located 37 miles east of Småland. Its location has long made Gotland a center for trade. Even at the height of the Roman Empire, Gotland was engaged in trade with continental Europe, and in Viking times was the main Baltic trading post. In the 1300s to 1400s, Gotland was a major trading post within the Hanseatic League.

Gotland lost its independence when invaded first by Germany and then by Denmark. It became Swedish in 1645. The island has a history of being a haven for refugees. During both World Wars many Eastern Europeans came across the sea in small boats fleeing the invading Germans and Russians.

The island has a limestone bedrock, fertile, lime-rich soil, and a mild climate. Sometimes called "the island of wind and roses," its flora and fauna are unique. Most animals, other than birds, have been brought over from the mainland, including sheep and other livestock, roe deer, hedgehogs, and hares.

Hedgehog

Gotland's economy has been built on trade, agriculture, and limestone quarries. Today tourism is a major industry. Visitors are intrigued by the unusual limestone formations known as *raukar* on the island's windswept northwest coast, created by surf wearing away the softer stone.

In the capital city of Visby, which is otherwise modern in every way, much medieval architecture can still be found, including a stone "city wall" built in the late thirteenth century that stretches nearly two miles and has forty-four watchtowers. In fact, remnants of the Middle Ages can be found all over the island and are celebrated at two annual festivals. In July the *Stångaspelen* (Pole Games) are held, with participants competing in Medieval Gotlandic fighting games, and in August "Medieval Week" takes place in Visby, with eight days of theater, music, jousting, and feasting. Lamb is a favorite regional dish, accompanied by fresh, locally grown vegetables.

Lamb with Dill *(Lamm med dillsås)*

1 (3-pound) lamb roast
8 cups water
1 tablespoon salt
6 whole peppercorns
several dill stalks

Gravy *(Sås)*:
1 tablespoon butter or margarine
3 tablespoons flour
2 cups stock
2 teaspoons sugar
3 teaspoons vinegar
2 tablespoons chopped dill

Rinse and dry the meat. Place in a pot and cover with water; bring to a boil. Skim. Add the salt, pepper, and dill stalks. Simmer slowly, covered, for about 2 hours. Remove meat to a platter; strain the stock and reserve 2 cups. Keep the meat warm while you make the gravy.

Gravy: Melt the butter in a saucepan, stir in the flour, and gradually add the meat stock, stirring constantly. Add the sugar, vinegar, and chopped dill.

Slice the meat and serve the gravy on the side. Serves 6.

Cheesy Vegetable Casserole *(Grönsaksgratäng)*

1 head cauliflower, cut into pieces
2 cups carrots, sliced
2 cups peas
2 tablespoons butter or margarine
3 tablespoons flour
2 cups light cream or milk
2 egg yolks, beaten
salt and pepper
4 tomatoes, peeled and sliced
1/2 cup grated cheese

Cook the cauliflower, carrots, and peas separately until tender. Drain. Arrange in a greased baking dish. Melt butter in a saucepan and stir in the flour until smooth. Add the cream gradually while stirring and cook slowly 10 minutes, stirring often. Set aside. Add egg yolks. Bring to a boil again, then remove from heat. Stir until thick and smooth. Season to taste.

Pour sauce over the vegetables and arrange tomato slices on top. Sprinkle grated cheese over everything. Broil about 10 minutes until brown.

American Professor Burns Weston of Iowa City, Iowa, took these photographs of a Gotland house with a thatched roof, left, and the historic wall at Visby, below.

ÖLAND

"I want to ask," said the old one, "if no one has had the desire to give wings to the windmills—so large that they could reach to heaven, so large that they could lift the whole island out of the sea and let it fly like a butterfly among butterflies."

—From *The Wonderful Adventures of Nils*
by Selma Lagerlöf

The island of Öland lies south of Gotland, off the shore of southern Småland. It is connected to the mainland by a 3.8-mile-long bridge built in the early 1970s.

When we visited in 1991, our first impression was of hundreds of windmills all across the landscape. Miles of sandy beaches stretch along the northern coastline, with rock formations similar to those on Gotland. Traveling inland one comes to the large nature preserve of Alvaret, where in spring and early summer, fields of brightly colored flowers bloom, including rare orchids found only here and on Gotland. Three hundred different species of birds sing their songs, and moose, deer, fox, and rabbit are common, as well as other types of wildlife. The scene is like a beautiful, tranquil garden.

Öland, however, has a long history of suffering at the hands of both man and nature. Throughout the Middle Ages the island suffered under corrupt monarchs, and endured marauding pirates and constant plagues. From 1569 until 1801 the island was used as a hunting retreat for the aristocracy. Local farmers were forced to kill all predatory animals to improve hunting conditions, but were not allowed to hunt any game themselves. Their crops suffered from all the deer and wild boar roaming around.

In the early 1800s conditions improved, but then in 1867–1868 came crop failure and famine, and mass Swedish emigration. More than thirteen thousand people left the tiny province—over a third of its total population.

Little remains to remind today's visitor of yesterday's hardships. Today Öland is a favorite destination for tourists and Swedish vacationers alike. Even the royal family has a summer home here.

Öland Castle Ruins **(Ölands borgruin)**

Öland Potato Dumplings *(Ölandskroppkakor)*

Potato dumplings are a specialty in Öland, as they are in the far northern province of Norrbotten. Here they are called kroppkakor, *which may be literally translated "body cakes." This recipe comes from Anne Fagerqvist, another of my relatives in Sweden. Anne and her family have a summer home on Öland.*

1 pound potatoes, raw
1/2 pound potatoes, cooked and mashed
1/2 cup flour
1/2 teaspoon salt
dash of pepper
salted water (1 teaspoon per quart)

Filling *(Fyllning)*:
1/4 pound precooked pork
2 tablespoons chopped onion
1/4 teaspoon ground allspice

Peel and grate the raw potatoes, then place them in a colander and press out the water. Mix with the mashed potatoes. Add flour, salt, and pepper, and work the dough until well blended. Cube the pork; brown together with onion and allspice.

Divide the dough into six to eight equal, round balls. Make a cavity in each ball, fill with pork mixture, and press together, concealing the filling. Place in boiling salted water and cook about 30 minutes. Serve immediately with butter and lingonberry jam or with gravy. Serves 3 to 4.

STOCKHOLM

"What city did we fly over just now?" he asked. "I don't know what human beings have named it," said Dunfin. "We gray geese call it the 'City that Floats on Water.' "

—From *The Further Adventures of Nils Holgersson*
by Selma Lagerlöf

The city of Stockholm is built to a large extent on islands, where Lake Mälaren meets the Baltic Sea. Everywhere one looks are water, bridges, and boats. Great ocean liners mingle with small ferries, fishing boats, and pleasure craft.

In Gamla Stan, the "old city," one finds narrow passageways, quaint shops, and apartments that have been renovated and are in great demand. Markets flourish in the heart of town, selling fresh produce, fish, and flowers. Stately churches with towering steeples co-exist with modern skyscrapers, offices, and trendy shopping centers. An efficient subway system connects the central city with the suburbs.

Tourists enjoy watching the daily "changing of the guard" ceremony at the Royal Palace, which, no longer the royal residence, is now Sweden's largest and most-visited museum. Since 1981 the king and his family have lived at Drottningholm Palace on the outskirts of the city.

Another place that tourists, as well as natives, like to visit is Skansen, a spacious outdoor museum in the heart of Stockholm. Here, three thousand acres of hills, woods, lakes, and fields reproduce Sweden in miniature. Examples of typical buildings from various regions and eras can be seen, and even regional plant and animal life have been faithfully reproduced. There is also an outdoor theater, from which programs are telecast nationwide during the summer season.

There are many fine restaurants in and around Stockholm, specializing in every type of cuisine, from Asian to Zulu. At Stadshuskällaren (City Hall Cellar), the meals are prepared each year for the Nobel Prize Award festivities, and in the magnificent Blue Hall, the banquet is served.

The Changing of the Guards

This scene, a tourist favorite, was photographed by Mansor Kia, Diana's husband, when they were in Sweden.

Stockholm City Hall,
Site of the Nobel Banquets

THE NOBEL AWARDS CEREMONY

When Swedish chemist, inventor, and philanthropist Alfred Nobel (1833–1896) died, he left behind something more than the formula for dynamite and his $9 million fortune; he left a legacy for humankind.

In his will, Nobel decreed that the major portion of his estate be set aside as a fund to establish yearly prizes for merit in the fields of physics, chemistry, literature, world peace, and medicine or physiology. The prizes should go, in Nobel's words, "to those persons who shall have contributed most materially to the benefit of mankind during the year immediately preceding." He expressly ordered that no consideration whatever be paid to the nationality of the recipients, only that they be the most deserving.

The first prizes were awarded on December 10, 1901, at the Grand Hotel in Stockholm. There were seven recipients and fewer than one hundred fifty guests, all male. These days the prizes are presented by Sweden's King Carl XVI Gustaf on the stage of the Stockholm Concert Hall, and the guest list has grown to over twelve hundred. After the award ceremony, guests are taken by limousine or bus to Stockholm's City Hall and treated to a sumptuous banquet.

Visitors to Stockholm can stop in at the Stadshuskällaren (City Hall Cellar) Restaurant any day and order a meal from any year's banquet from the Nobel Menu. For example, say: "I'll have the 1921 Einstein menu, please," and you'll be served fillet of turbot a la Walewska, saddle of lamb with vegetables and Choron sauce, and pears with vanilla ice cream and raspberry sauce.

The Stadshuskällaren Restaurant in Stockholm contributed the following recipes, from the 1996 banquet, and are used with permission. I have edited some of the directions for clarity. Also, measurements have been converted from metric to English. All are portioned for four servings.

Lobster and Vegetables in Aspic
(Aladåb med hummer och grönsaker)

1 quart lobster stock
2 egg whites
1/4 cup minced vegetables (like carrots, celery, onion, fennel)
2 tablespoons sauterne
2 teaspoons brandy
salt
cayenne pepper
approx. 2-1/2 tablespoons gelatin (follow package directions)

1 boiled lobster
2 tomatoes
1/4 leek
2 artichokes
lemon
lettuce leaves

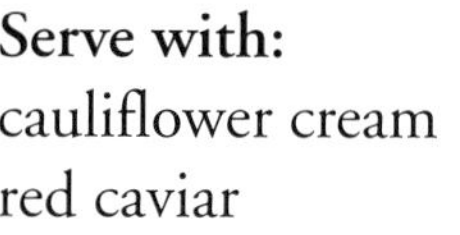

Serve with:
cauliflower cream
red caviar

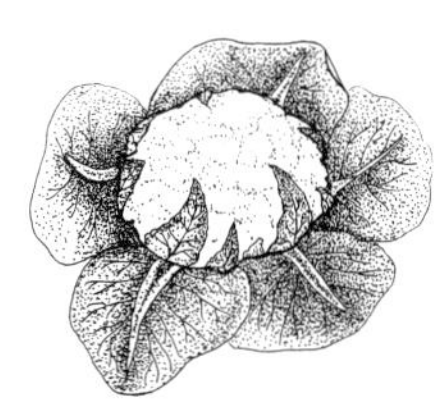

Cauliflower

Clarify the stock. This may be done best by making it the day before, then refrigerating it overnight so that the fat rises to the top and solidifies, and can easily be removed. Pour the cold stock into a saucepan. Lightly whip the egg white and pour it in. Add the minced vegetables.

Simmer slowly, stirring along the bottom of the pan with a wooden spoon, so that the egg white is moved around in the stock. Gradually, as the liquid grows hotter, the egg white will coagulate, envelope the particles that cloud the stock, and float on the surface. Remove these impurities from the surface and strain the stock twice. Bring to a boil and skim carefully. Add the sauterne, brandy, salt, and a pinch or two of cayenne pepper.

Measure the amount of finished stock and calculate how much gelatin will be needed. Dissolve the gelatin in the hot stock, stirring constantly. Leave to cool. The stock should be as cold as possible, although not firm, when it is poured over the lobster and vegetables.

Clean the lobster and dry it well. Cut into pieces of about 1/2 inch.

Blanch, peel, and deseed the tomatoes. Cut them into 1/2-inch pieces. Cut the leeks into pieces of the same size. Parboil them for a minute or so in well-salted water and then rinse them under cold running water.

Remove the leaves and the "choke," or hairy center, from the artichokes. Rub the artichokes with lemon and boil them for 6 or 7 minutes in generously salted water. Cut them into pieces.

Portion out the lobster into four individual ring molds. (If ring molds are not available, use any individual-sized mold.) Add the tomato pieces and then the leeks and artichokes. Pour on the stock, which should be as cool as possible.

Refrigerate the molds overnight. When ready to serve, dip the molds into warm water and turn them out onto a bed of lettuce leaves on four plates. Serve with the cauliflower cream in the center, or on the side, and red caviar.

Cauliflower Cream *(Blomkålssås)*

1 cauliflower head, approx. 1/2 pound (do not include root)
3/4 cup whipping cream
1/4 cup milk
salt and white pepper
2 tablespoons *créme fraiche*

Pick or cut off the cauliflower florets, rinse them well, and drain. Place the cauliflower in a saucepan; add the cream and milk. Simmer carefully until the cauliflower is soft.

Mix to a smooth cream in a blender. Add salt and pepper to taste. Allow to cool. Stir in the *créme fraiche* just before serving.

The Stockholm Harbor

Minced Guinea Fowl with Roasted Root Vegetables
(Pärlhöna med stekta rotgrönsaker)

2 guinea fowl of 2 to 2-1/2 pounds each
2/3 cup chicken stock
2 tablespoons barley
2 teaspoons common parsley (the kind with flat, smooth leaves)
1/2 apple
1 small onion
1/4 cup mushrooms
salt and pepper
1 pound of root vegetables such as carrots, turnips, celeriac root, and *mange-tout* (beets)

Cut off the legs (drumsticks). Remove the skin from each bird carefully so that it remains as much intact as possible. Cut off the thigh meat and breast meat and set this aside.

To make the chicken stock, pour about 3 cups of water over the bones, legs, and wings and add a few chopped vegetables. Simmer for long enough to make a stock. (You will use just over half a cup in this recipe and may use the remaining 2 cups or so in the citrus sauce recipe that follows. Commercially prepared stock, canned or made from cubes, may be used instead, if desired.)

Mix the barley with 1/2 cup of the chicken stock and simmer slowly for about 30 minutes. Allow to cool. Mix the chopped parsley with 2 tablespoons cold stock and then stir this into the barley mixture.

Preheat oven to 350°. Dice the meat from the thighs and set this aside.

Peel and core the apple and cut into small cubes. Peel and chop the onion. Cut the mushrooms into pieces.

Sauté the apple, onion, and mushrooms separately and allow them to cool, then mix them with the thigh meat and the barley mixture. Season with a little salt and pepper.

Spread out the skin and place the sliced breast meat on top, overlapping the slices. Add the barley mixture and more salt and pepper, if desired. Roll tightly, then wrap the roll in aluminum foil that has been sprayed with a nonstick spray. Bake the roll in the oven 30 minutes. Remove from the oven and set aside to cool.

Peel the root vegetables and cut them into cubes, triangles, and batons. Parboil them until they are just *al dente* and then rinse them in cold water.

Note: All of the above steps may be done ahead of time, even the day before.

Just before serving, slice the roll into medallions and fry them until they become golden brown. Brown the vegetables in butter and add salt and pepper to taste. Serve with puréed potatoes and citrus sauce.

Puréed Almond Potatoes *(Mandelpotatismos)*

1-1/2 pounds almond potatoes or other small, yellow potatoes
2/3 cup milk
6 tablespoons butter
1 to 2 tablespoons chopped fresh thyme*
salt and pepper

Peel and boil the potatoes. Drain and rice them through a potato press. Heat the milk. Add the milk, chunks of butter, and thyme and mix to make a smooth, fluffy purée. Add salt and pepper to taste.

*It is essential to use fresh thyme in this dish. If fresh thyme is not available, better to use fresh parsley or leave out the herb altogether.

Citrus Sauce *(Citronsås)*

1/4 lime
1/4 lemon
1/4 orange
1 onion, chopped
1 teaspoon sugar
3 ounces white port
2 cups chicken stock
1-1/2 cups whipping cream
3 tablespoons butter
salt and pepper

Grate the peel of the citrus fruits. Squeeze the juice. Sauté the onion in a little butter together with the sugar and the grated citrus peel. Add the citrus juices and the port. Reduce until most of the liquid has disappeared. Add the stock and reduce to make the concentration rich and tasty. Add the cream and reduce even further until the consistency is just right. Mix in the butter and season to taste. Strain the sauce before serving.

Arctic Raspberry Dessert *(Arktisk hallonefterrätt)*

Every Nobel dinner ends with a dessert featuring ice cream in some form.

1 pint vanilla ice cream
1/2 pint raspberry sorbet

Leave the vanilla ice cream out of the freezer just long enough for it to soften, so that it is spreadable without being runny. Cover the inside of a bowl with cling film. (Make sure the bowl is just big enough to hold the 1-1/2 pints.) Spread out the ice cream on the base and along the walls, leaving a cavity in the middle.

Place the bowl in the freezer for an hour or so, until the ice cream becomes firm. Leave the sorbet to soften as well, but make sure it doesn't become too soft, which can happen quickly. Fill the cavity in the ice cream with sorbet and cover everything with cling film.

Put the bowl back into the freezer. Take it out again about half an hour before serving and turn the mold out onto a serving platter. You may garnish the dish with berries or fruit. Serve with petit fours or cookies.

Hand-painted Roosters by Grannas A. Olssons Hemslöjd AB, Nusnäs, Sweden, from Bergquist Imports, Inc., Cloquet, Minnesota

HERE CHICK, CHICK, CHICK ...
(and other things too good to miss!)

In my search for regional specialties, I came to notice something missing: chicken! Not one province listed a chicken dish among its traditional favorites. The reason for this is unclear, since we know that eggs and egg dishes have always been popular. Nevertheless, in "Swedish" Stanton, Iowa, chicken is eaten regularly, and recipes have been passed down in families for generations. I have included a few of my own favorites. Other examples of standard Swedish fare that didn't turn up in any specific province are *pytt i panna* (hash), *biff a la Lindström* (beef ala Lindström), and *Svenska pannkakor* (Swedish pancakes).

Roasted Spring Chicken *(Stekt vårkyckling)*

2 tablespoons butter or
 margarine, divided
1 bunch of parsley, without stems
1 young chicken
1 teaspoon salt
dash of pepper
1 cup chicken bouillon

Gravy *(Sås)*:
1 tablespoon flour
1/2 cup milk or cream
pan drippings

Melt 1 tablespoon of the butter. Chop the parsley and mix it with the melted butter, then stuff the cavity of the bird with this. Sew the cavity shut. Melt the remaining butter in a pan and brown the bird on all sides. Season with salt and pepper. Add bouillon and simmer, covered, for about 45 minutes.

Remove the chicken and keep warm while you make the gravy. Mix the flour with a small amount of milk until smooth; gradually add more milk, then stir this into the pan drippings. Cook about 5 minutes. Serves 2 to 4.

Chicken Fricassee with Rice *(Kycklingfrikassé med ris)*

1 chicken
4 cups water
1 teaspoon lemon juice
salt
pepper
1 bay leaf
1/4 cup chopped onion
1 cup white rice
2-1/2 cups water
fresh parsley, for garnish

Sauce *(Sås)*:
1 tablespoon butter or margarine
1 tablespoon flour
1 cup chicken bouillon
1/4 cup cream
1 egg yolk, beaten
salt
pepper

Cut the chicken into pieces. Remove skin and extra fat; rinse and dry. Place in a pot, cover with water, and bring to a boil. Skim; add the lemon juice, spices, and onion. Simmer slowly, covered, about 2 hours.

When the chicken has been cooking for about 1-1/4 hours, make the rice in a separate pot. Bring the water to a boil, stir in the rice, and simmer, covered, for about 30 minutes, until water is absorbed and rice is tender.

When the chicken is done, remove from pot, set aside, and keep warm while you make the sauce. Melt the butter, stir in the flour, and gradually add the bouillon. Stir this into the pan drippings, cook about 10 minutes, add the cream, and heat through. Remove from heat. Stir in the beaten egg yolk and season with salt and pepper.

Arrange the rice and chicken pieces on a serving platter. Pour a little of the sauce over; serve the rest on the side. Garnish with fresh parsley sprigs. Serves 4.

Chicken with Mushrooms *(Kyckling med svamp)*

2 skinless chicken breasts, halved (4 pieces)
1/4 cup white wine
1 cup chicken bouillon
1 small clove garlic, minced
1 teaspoon salt
1 tablespoon flour
1/2 teaspoon paprika
1-1/2 cups cream or milk
1 cup cooked or canned mushrooms

Place chicken pieces in a pan. Add wine, bouillon, and garlic and simmer slowly for about 1 hour.

Mix the salt, flour, and paprika with a little cream, stirring until smooth. Gradually add the rest of the cream, then stir this into the broth. Add mushrooms; stir until thickened. Adjust seasoning. Serve with rice or potatoes and green vegetables. Serves 4.

Hash *(Pytt i panna)*

2 tablespoons butter or margarine
1 to 2 onions, chopped
2 cups leftover meat, ground or chopped
3 cups cooked, diced potatoes
salt and pepper
4 eggs
sliced tomato

Melt the butter; sauté the onions until tender. Add the meat and potatoes; brown. Season to taste. Fry or poach the eggs. Serve the hash topped with eggs and garnished with tomato slices.

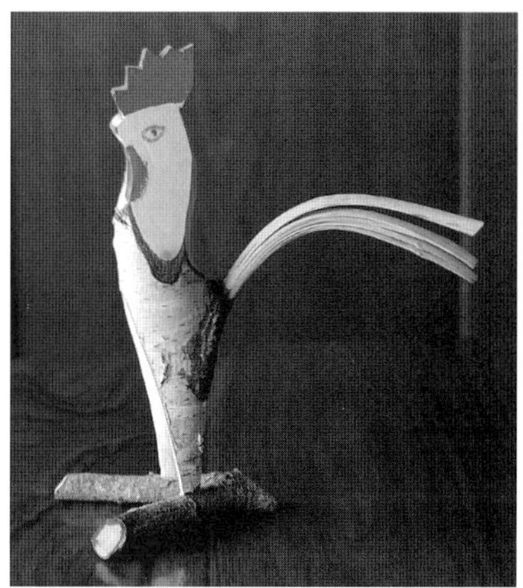

Swedish birch woodcarving of a saucy wooden rooster

Beef a la Lindström *(Biff á la Lindström)*

1-1/4 pounds ground chuck or round
2 boiled potatoes, mashed
2 egg yolks
1/2 cup cream or milk
2 pickled beets, diced
1-1/2 tablespoons minced onion
2 tablespoons mushrooms, diced
salt and white pepper
2 to 3 tablespoons butter or margarine

Combine the meat, potatoes, eggs, and cream. Mix in the beets, onions, and mushrooms gently with a fork. Season. Shape into patties. Heat butter in a skillet. Brown patties. Serve with fried potatoes.

Beets

Swedish Pancakes *(Svenska pannkakor)*

Adapted from the Swedish Dairy Institute

3/4 cup flour
1/2 teaspoon salt
2 cups milk
3 eggs
2 tablespoons melted butter
lingonberry syrup or jam

Blend the flour, salt, and a little of the milk to a smooth, lump-free consistency. Add the rest of the milk, eggs, and melted butter. (Be sure to beat very well.) Fry as thin pancakes about 8 inches in diameter. Brown very lightly. These are very thin, and it may take a little practice to turn them successfully. A nonstick griddle works best. Serve with lingonberry syrup or jam.

HOLIDAYS AND FESTIVALS

WALPURGIS NIGHT *(VALBORGSMÄSSOAFTON)*

"Yes, this is surely spring," thought all the animal folk.
"Winter chill has vanished. The fires of spring burn over the earth."

—From *The Wonderful Adventures of Nils*
by Selma Lagerlöf

On the last day of April, Swedes celebrate the end of winter and the coming of spring with bonfires and singing. In ancient times they lit bonfires to frighten away witches and evil spirits. This also served the more practical purpose of frightening away predatory animals before cattle and sheep were put out to spring pasture.

The old superstitions are gone, as are the wolves. Today the bonfires (and sometimes fireworks) are just a joyous celebration of the return of light and warmth.

Students at Uppsala, Lund, and other universities put on their white high school graduation caps for the festivities, which include singing songs such as *Sköna Maj* (Beautiful May) to welcome spring. In the past this was done by all-male choral groups, but today women join in as well.

After the bonfires, singing, and dancing, everyone is ready for the feasting, which will surely include *gravad lax med senapssås* (marinated salmon with mustard sauce).

Sheep

Marinated Salmon with Mustard Sauce
(Gravad lax med senapssås)

1 teaspoon whole white peppercorns
1 tablespoon salt
1/4 cup sugar
3/4 cup finely chopped dill
2 pounds salmon fillet

Sauce:
1 tablespoon yellow mustard
1 tablespoon brown mustard
1 tablespoon red wine vinegar
2 teaspoons honey
3/4 cup vegetable oil
1 tablespoon fresh chopped dill, or 1 teaspoon dried, chopped dill
salt and pepper

Grind the peppercorns and combine with the salt, sugar, and dill. Remove the skin from the salmon; sprinkle the spices onto both sides. Place the fish in a sealed bag or covered dish. Refrigerate about 48 hours. Turn several times. Pour off any liquid and wipe the fish clean. Cut into thin slices. Serve raw.

Combine sauce ingredients. Pour sauce over the salmon, or serve on the side. Serves 6.

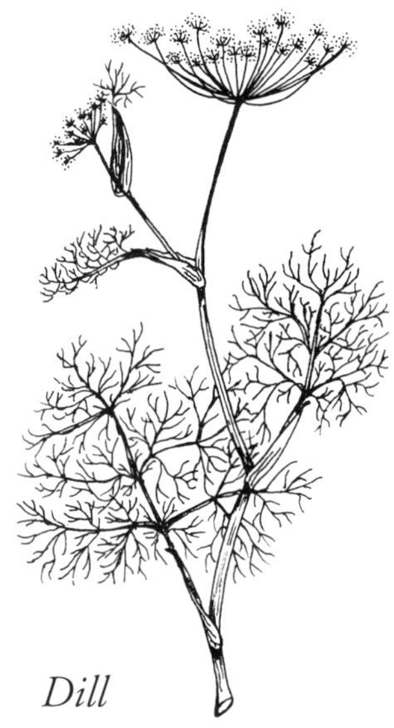
Dill

EASTER *(PÅSK)*

He remembered that this was Easter eve. "It is tonight that all the witches come home from Blakulla," thought he, and laughed to himself. For he was just a little afraid of both the sea nymph and the elf, but he didn't believe in witches the least little bit.

—From *The Wonderful Adventures of Nils*
by Selma Lagerlöf

Old superstition had it that witches and other evil spirits were especially active around the holidays, and in an effort to chase them away, people prayed, sang, and lit fires. In some of the western provinces of Sweden one may still see bonfires at Easter, although in most of the country this is more common on *Walpurgis* Night.

Today those "witches" are remembered in a manner similar to the American practice of Halloween. On Easter Eve, little girls wearing witch costumes go door-to-door handing out cards and drawings in return for treats or money.

The Easter feast begins and ends with eggs, and there is a historical reason for this. During the forty days of Lent, faithful Christians were expected to fast, which meant eating no meat, poultry, dairy products, or eggs—and this at the beginning of spring when hens had begun to lay a great many eggs!

In Sweden, as in other parts of Europe and America, Easter eggs are dyed and decorated. The old methods of using natural products for coloring like onion skin, saffron, coffee, fennel, and beet root are still followed by many traditional Swedes on this occasion.

Roast lamb is a rather newly adopted custom, as is the Easter Bunny.

Eggs in Green Sauce *(Ägg i grön sås)*

4 hard-cooked eggs, shelled
8 tomato slices
1/2 cup small, cooked, shelled shrimp

Sauce:
1/2 cup mayonnaise
1/2 cup whipped cream
2 tablespoons strained spinach (baby food works well)
1 tablespoon finely chopped parsley

Slice shelled eggs in half lengthwise. Lay the tomato slices on a plate and place the egg halves, yolk side down, on the tomato slices. Combine sauce ingredients and pour over the eggs. Top with the shrimp.

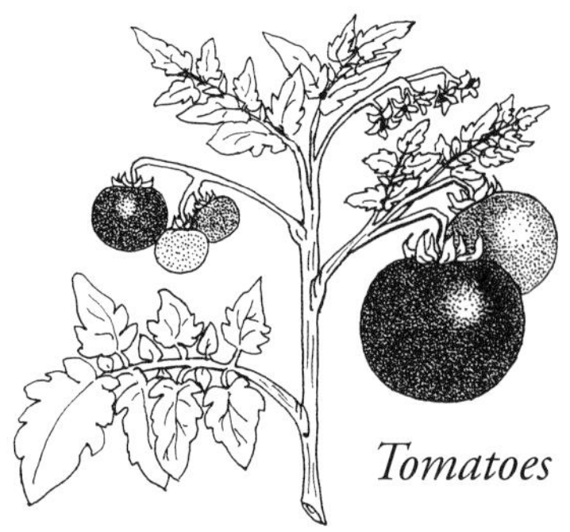

Tomatoes

Eggs in Spinach Stew *(Ägg i stuvad spenat)*

1 package frozen spinach, thawed
1/4 cup grated onion
2 tablespoons margarine
1 tablespoon flour
1 cup milk
salt and pepper
4 hard-cooked eggs, shelled
6 bacon slices, fried and cut into pieces

Preheat oven to 450°. Sauté the spinach and onion in the margarine. Sprinkle with flour and stir in the milk. Bring to a boil, stirring constantly. Simmer a few minutes. Season to taste with salt and pepper. Pour into a greased oven dish.

Slice shelled eggs in half lengthwise. Arrange the egg halves, yolk side up, on the spinach mixture. Top with chopped bacon. Bake until heated through.

Omelet with Asparagus *(Omelett med sparris)*

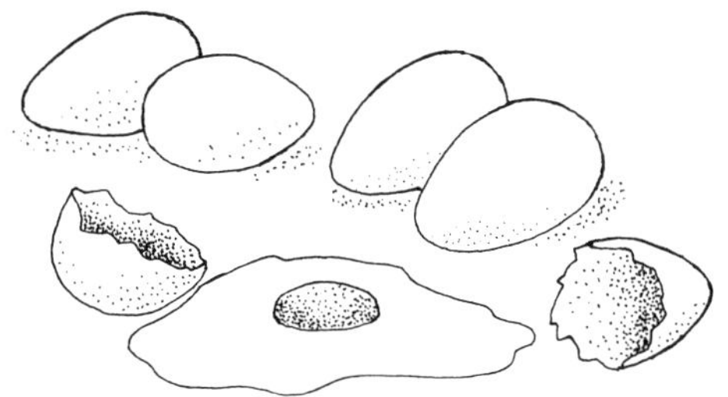

6 eggs, separated
1-1/4 cups light cream
1/2 teaspoon salt
1/2 teaspoon sugar

Sauce:
6 to 8 fresh asparagus spears
3 tablespoons butter or margarine
3 tablespoons flour
salt and pepper
1-1/2 cups milk
1 egg yolk, lightly beaten

Preheat oven to 350°. Beat the egg yolks slightly. Mix in cream, salt, and sugar. Beat the egg whites until stiff and fold into the yolk mixture. Pour into a greased baking dish. Bake 15 to 20 minutes until golden brown.

Sauce: Steam the asparagus until tender. Drain. Melt butter in a saucepan; stir in the flour, salt, and pepper, then gradually stir in the milk. Cook over medium heat until sauce thickens, stirring constantly. Reduce heat to very low and continue to cook for 10 minutes, stirring occasionally. Stir in egg yolk and cook for 2 more minutes. Add asparagus. Heat through. Pour over omelet to serve.

Roast Lamb *(Lammstek)*

1 lamb roast, about 2-1/2 pounds
1/2 teaspoon salt
dash pepper
1/4 teaspoon paprika
1/2 cup bouillon
1/2 cup dry white wine
1 tablespoon tomato paste
1 clove garlic, minced

Gravy *(Sås)*:
pan drippings
1 tablespoon flour
1/2 cup water
1/4 cup cream

Preheat the oven to 350°. Rub the meat with salt, pepper, and paprika. Brown on all sides; cover with foil. Place in the oven. Blend bouillon, wine, tomato paste, and minced garlic. Use liquid for basting meat occasionally during roasting. Roast about 1 to 1-1/2 hours or until meat thermometer registers 150 to 160°. Remove to serving platter and keep warm. Skim extra grease from drippings and strain them into a saucepan. Heat to boiling. Dissolve flour in a small amount of water and stir into the drippings. Add cream and heat. Serve with roasted potatoes and steamed vegetables. Serves 6.

Malmö Dancers

MIDSUMMER *(MIDSOMMAR)*

The sun stood still and just beamed and smiled.

—From *The Further Adventures of Nils Holgersson*
by Selma Lagerlöf

If there is one celebration that is uniquely Swedish, it is the festival of *Midsommar*. Swedes are well known as sun worshippers; it's only natural that the summer solstice, the longest day of the year, should be celebrated in a big way. This is an outdoor event, with everyone who is able to do so heading out into the countryside.

At the center of these celebrations stands the flower-bedecked *Midsommar* pole, or *majstång*. In America, and in many parts of Europe, "Maypoles" are associated with the arrival of May. In the old Swedish language, however, to *maja* (a verb) means to "decorate with leaves and greenery." In Sweden, the *majstång* is a decorated *Midsommar* pole, which has nothing to do with the month of May.

The province of Dalarna is well known for its traditional and colorful *Midsommar* activities, but every town and village throughout the entire country celebrates, and there is sure to be singing, dancing, and feasting far into the night. Traditional costume is optional.

New potatoes boiled and sprinkled with dill are a must, along with pickled herring served in various ways. There should be fresh fruit, ice cream, and a plentiful variety of other tasty treats. Naturally, everything is served and eaten out-of-doors!

Potatoes and dill

Midsommar

Midsummer Dancers (Midsommardans)

Pickled Herring with Eggs *(Sill med ägg)*

- 4 pickled herring fillets
- 2 hard-cooked eggs, chopped
- 1 bunch dill, chopped fine
- 1 onion, chopped
- 2 pickled beets, chopped
- 1/2 cup butter or margarine

Cut the herring fillets in 1/2-inch pieces and arrange them on a platter. Sprinkle the eggs, dill, onion, and beets over the herrings. Melt the butter in a skillet over high heat, stirring constantly, until it is browned. Pour over the herring dish just before serving.

Strawberry-Rhubarb Compote
(Jordgubbs-och rabarberkompott)

1 pound rhubarb
1-1/2 cups sugar
1/4 cup water
2 tablespoons cornstarch
2 pints strawberries

Sauce:
2 cups light cream
1/2 cup sugar
6 egg yolks
1 teaspoon vanilla

Peel skin from rhubarb and cut into 1/2-inch slices. Add sugar and water; stir, cover, and bring slowly to a simmer. Simmer 7 to 10 minutes until rhubarb is soft.

Dissolve cornstarch in a little water and add to the mix. Wash and cut the strawberries in half. Add them to the mix.

Sauce: Mix the cream and sugar and bring to a boil. Beat the egg yolks well and add them to the sauce. Bring almost to a boil again, stirring constantly. When sauce thickens, remove from heat and stir in the vanilla.

Refrigerate both the fruit compote and the sauce and serve cold.

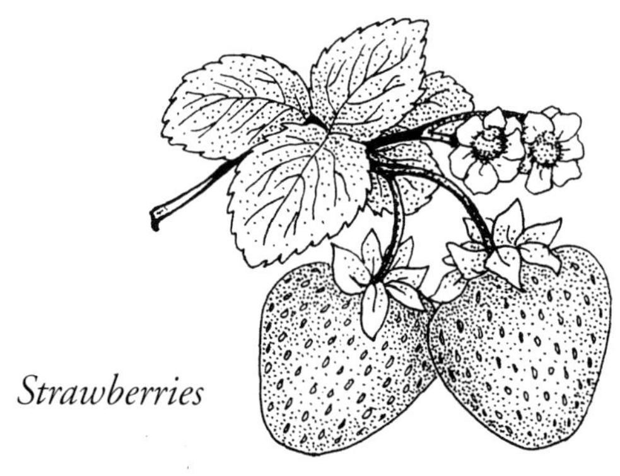

Strawberries

Pineapple-Strawberry Torte *(Ananas-och jordgubbstårta)*

My cousin Inge Eriksson made this for us when he visited Stanton, Iowa, at Midsommar *2003. What a special treat.*

2 (9-inch) layers of yellow cake
canned, crushed pineapple
strawberry preserves
whipped cream (should be firm)
fresh strawberries

Split the cake layers horizontally so that you have four thin layers. Spread crushed pineapple on two of the half-layers, and spread strawberry preserves liberally on the third. Stack the layers like this: cake, crushed pineapple, cake, strawberry preserves, cake, crushed pineapple, cake. Spread whipped cream generously over the top and sides, then decorate with strawberries. Be creative. Slice and enjoy!

Pineapple

Dining on Crayfish (Kräftskiva) *in Malmö*

One of the first crayfish parties was hosted in 1562 by Erik XIV, son of Gustav Vasa. By the middle of the 1800s, *kräftskivor* were popular nationwide on August evenings with "pyramids of red crayfish boiled in dill."

—From the *ASI Posten,* 2004, published by The American Swedish Institute

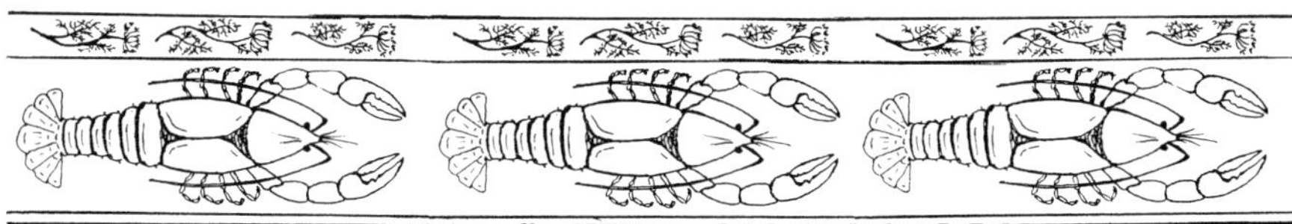

CRAYFISH PARTIES *(KRÄFTSKIVOR)*

In August, when the sun starts to set earlier following a period of long white summer nights, Sweden explodes with crayfish parties. We decorate our porches with colored lanterns and sometimes dress up in crazy little paper hats and fill the tables with mountains of beautiful red crayfish decorated with dill flowers. You eat enormous amounts of crayfish and with it you drink beer and lots of aquavit *(snaps)*. Each time you propose a new toast you sing a new *"snaps-song,"* of which there is an extensive repertoire.

When I grew up in the 1940s people would go out to the local lake or stream with their cages to catch crayfish on the first day that fishing was allowed. Then the parties would follow. Today, most people buy their crayfish in the supermarket, but it is still after the allowed fishing date (generally after the first week of August) that the crayfish celebration explodes.

The reason there are no recipes is that everyone is expected to know the simple art of cooking crayfish. You boil them in a big pot of salted water with lots of dill stems in it. Then you let the crayfish cool off in the water and you eat them chilled.

In northern Sweden crayfish parties are often organized, instead, around fermented Baltic herring, which is served with chopped raw onions, hard bread, cheese, and special small potatoes *(mandelpotatis)*. The drinking pattern is the same as with the crayfish parties, and they take place at the same time of the year.

—Marta Cullberg Weston, Stockholm

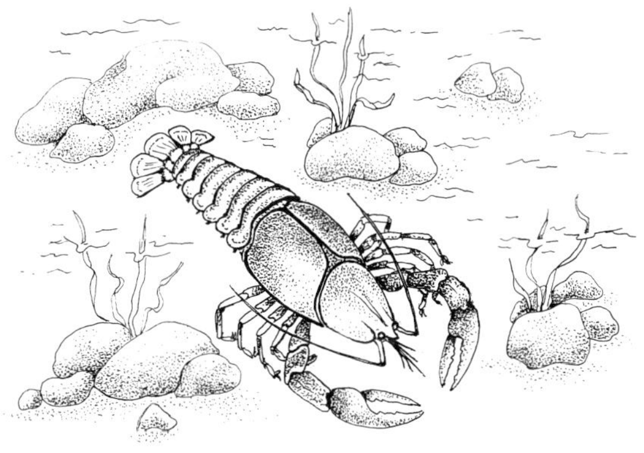

ADVENT & SANTA LUCIA DAY
(ADVENT OCH LUCIA)

Lucia Day, when the housemaid went about dressed in white with candles in her hair ...

—From *The Further Adventures of Nils Holgersson*
by Selma Lagerlöf

The Swedish Christmas season begins with the Advent star and candles shining in the windows of almost every home. One candle is lit the first Sunday in Advent, two the second Sunday, and so on through the four weeks leading up to Christmas.

In mid-December comes the very special Swedish celebration of Santa Lucia Day. Lucia was actually an Italian saint, born in Sicily in the third century AD when the Roman Empire was at the height of its power. She was a Christian, involved in charitable work. Legend has it that when she carried food to the poor and sick people huddled in dark catacombs, she tied candles to her head to light her way.

Lucia was engaged to marry a nobleman, but he insisted that she give up her "foolish" charitable activities, and she refused. Various stories are told about her "courage under fire." Some say she put out her own eyes to avoid the marriage and was miraculously given new ones. Easier to believe is that she gave away her dowry, and her intended groom angrily ordered her arrested. She was imprisoned and tortured, but would not be broken. Then, the legend says, attempts to drown or burn her at the stake failed, and the frustrated executioner had to resort to the sword. Her execution took place on December 13, AD 304, the shortest day of the year according to the old Viking calendar. Later, Lucia was declared a saint by the Catholic Church.

Viking traders brought the Lucia story back to Sweden, where she was quickly adopted. The vision of a virtuous maiden in a long, white gown, carrying food to the needy and wearing a crown of candles in her hair, was irresistible, all the more so as she came in winter's darkest night, bringing light and hope.

In 1529, after Martin Luther's Protestant Reformation, the celebration of saints in Sweden was forbidden, but it was hard for Swedes to give up two of their favorites, St. Nicholas and St. Lucia.

Today Lucia's legend lives on. Each year on December 13, in the predawn hours, it is re-enacted in homes all across Sweden. Young girls don the white gown with a red sash and the crown of candles (today battery-powered lights are more common, and safer), and carry trays of *kaffe* (coffee), *glögg* (hot spiced wine), *pepparkakor* (ginger snap cookies), and warm saffron buns called *lussekatter* ("Lucia cats"). They sing the traditional Lucia song as they serve their families. That day there is feasting in the house, ending with a little extra portion of goodies for everyone, including the household animals.

This popular celebration has grown over time. Today every town, village, and school selects their own "Lucia Queen," and Sweden's official Lucia is chosen in a nationally televised event.

"St. Lucia" with Children

Lucia Saffron Buns *(Lussekatter)*

1 cup milk
1/2 cup soft butter or margarine
3/4 cup sugar
1 teaspoon salt
1/2 teaspoon powdered saffron
3/4 cup warm water
2 packages active dry yeast
6-1/2 cups sifted white flour, divided
2 eggs
1/2 cup raisins plus more for decoration
1/2 cup ground blanched almonds
egg yolk mixed with 1 tablespoon water

In a small saucepan heat the milk until it is almost, but not quite, boiling. Remove from heat and add the butter, stirring until melted, then add the sugar, salt, and saffron. Cool to lukewarm. Pour the warm water into a large bowl and add the yeast, stirring until dissolved. Add the milk mixture.

Add 3 cups flour and mix until smooth. Stir in the eggs, raisins, and almonds. Gradually add the rest of the flour.

Turn the dough out onto a lightly floured surface. Cover and allow to rest for about 10 minutes, then knead the dough until smooth. Keep the dough lightly coated with flour to prevent sticking.

Place in a lightly greased bowl. Turn to bring up the greased side. Cover with a towel and allow to rise in a warm place until doubled in size, about 1 to 1-1/2 hours.

Turn out again onto a lightly floured surface and gently knead. Divide into thirds and roll out each piece into a 10-inch square. Cut in half to make two 10 x 5" rectangles, then cut each rectangle into twelve 5-inch-long strips. Roll each strip to the size of a 6-inch pencil.

On a lightly greased cookie sheet, make an X with two strips, then coil each of the ends. Place a raisin in the center of each coil. (Other shapes can be made with the strips as desired.) Cover with a towel and allow to rise in a warm place about 45 minutes.

Preheat oven to 400°. Brush buns with egg yolk mixed with water and bake 12 to 15 minutes or until golden brown. Makes 36 buns.

Lucia Buns and Variations

Drawn by Esther Feske

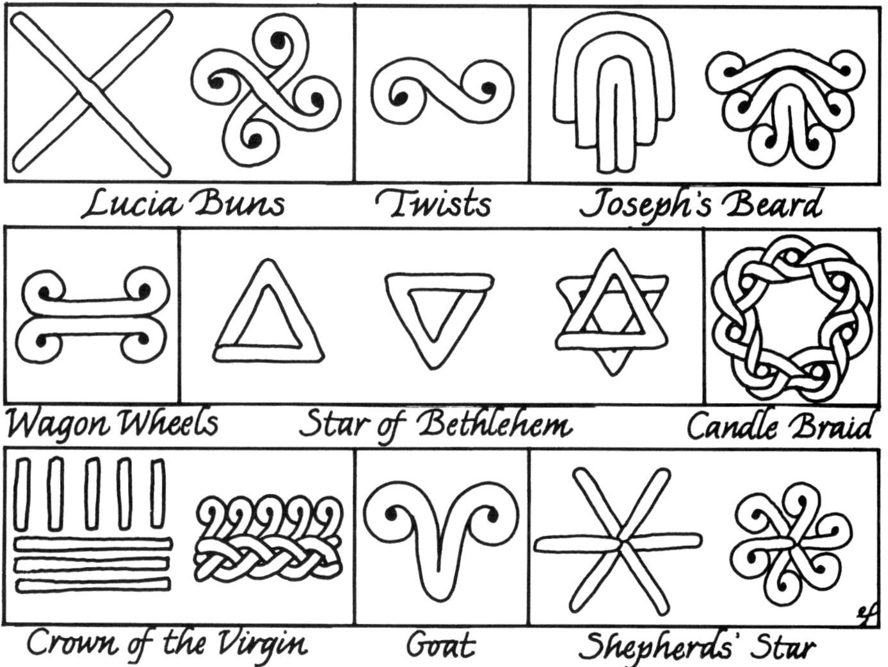

These are ways to shape saffron dough (or any other yeast dough) for Lucia buns. Raisins accent the curls. Balls of foil hold space for candles during the rising and baking of the candle braid.

Spiced Punch *(Glögg)*

1 cinnamon stick
20 whole cloves
1-1/2 teaspoons cardamom
1/4 teaspoon ginger
grated peel of half an orange
1 bottle red wine (about 3 cups)
1-1/2 cups port wine or 3/4 cup whiskey
1/2 teaspoon vanilla
1/3 cup brown sugar
1/2 cup blanched and sliced or slivered almonds
1 cup raisins

Mix the spices and orange peel with the wine (or whiskey if that is used) and let stand at least 24 hours, or up to several days.

Heat the mixture but do not boil. Stir in vanilla and brown sugar. Strain the liquid, then add the almonds and raisins. Serve warm.

Variation, non-alcoholic: Use 3 cups black currant juice and 1-1/2 cups apple juice instead of the wine and whiskey. Omit brown sugar.

Gingersnaps *(Pepparkakor)*

by Ester Harkins, my Swedish teacher

1/2 cup butter
3/4 cup sugar
1 egg, well beaten
1-1/2 teaspoons dark corn syrup
1-1/2 cups sifted flour
1 teaspoon baking soda
1-1/2 teaspoons ginger
1 teaspoon cinnamon
1/4 teaspoon cloves
sliced almonds (optional)

Mix the butter and sugar together until smooth and creamy. Add the egg and corn syrup. Beat well. Add in the dry ingredients, except the almonds, gradually and mix very well. Chill in the refrigerator several hours.

Preheat oven to 375°. Roll out small amounts at a time on a lightly floured surface. Keep the dough cold; roll thin.

Cut out shapes. Bake on ungreased cookie sheet for 6 to 8 minutes. Top with sliced almonds if desired.

CHRISTMAS *(JUL)*

For now they must brew the Christmas ale, steep the Christmas fish in lye, and do their Christmas baking and Christmas scouring.

—From *The Further Adventures of Nils Holgersson*
by Selma Lagerlöf

Christmas in Sweden, as elsewhere, is a mixture of old and new, sacred and secular, of traditions adopted from and shared with other countries, and of those uniquely Swedish.

In centuries past the two weeks preceding Christmas would have been spent fasting; now they seem to be spent shopping! Housecleaning is still a must, and homes today are decorated even more elaborately than in the past. The *julgran* (Christmas tree), which originated in Germany and spread to Sweden as well as to other parts of Scandinavia, Europe, and America in the 1800s, is found in nearly every home and usually decorated with straw ornaments and candle-shaped lights.

Baking is done in advance of the big day; there must be plenty of bread and sweets on hand for family and guests. It is customary to prepare at least seven kinds of cookies, as well as homemade candy.

The high point of Christmas in Sweden occurs on Christmas Eve. Preparation of the evening meal begins in the morning, and at noon everyone gathers in the kitchen for *dopp i grytan* (dip in the kettle). This involves dipping pieces of bread into the broth left from cooking the ham and sausage. The bread may be *vörtbröd*, made with malt extract, or *limpa*, sweetened with molasses, orange peel, and/or raisins, or perhaps polar flatbread.

Gifts are exchanged on Christmas Eve, either before or after dinner. These are called *julklappar* (Christmas knocks), recalling an old custom in which the gift giver would deposit a gift at the door, knock, and then run away. Usually, the giver would be caught and brought in for refreshments.

Nowadays, when there are children in the household, gifts are usually delivered by the *jultomten* (Christmas elf), who may be an uncle or friend of the family in costume. He comes to the door and asks, *"Finns det några snälla barn här?"* ("Are there any nice children here?") And, of course, the answer is always, "Yes!"

The evening meal begins with crispbread and cheese and the traditional *smörgåsbord*, which translates literally "sandwich table" but is much more lavish. There are cold dishes like pickled herring, jellied salmon loaf, and fresh raw vegetables, and *småvarmt* (small warm dishes) like *köttbullar* (meatballs) and *Janssons frestelse* (Jansson's temptation).

Ham, sausage, and boiled potatoes are sure to be served, but no traditional Christmas feast would be complete without lutfisk! This is dried stockfish that is prepared by soaking the fish first in lye and then in water, a tedious and foul-smelling process that today may be avoided by buying the finished product already prepared. Lutfisk is served hot with butter, cream sauce, or mustard sauce and plenty of salt and pepper. *Risgrynsgröt* (rice pudding) may be served for dessert. A single almond is hidden in the pudding, and the one who receives it can expect good fortune in the coming year.

Pets and livestock are given an extra ration of food on Christmas Eve, and even the wild birds are remembered by tying up a grain sheaf on a pole for them to enjoy. One must also not forget to set out a little bowl of pudding for the *tomten*, who might otherwise be displeased and make mischief! It may be that he shares it with the fox or the neighbor's cat, but in any case the pudding will surely be gone by morning.

Christmas church service, called *julotta*, is held early in the morning of Christmas day, after which a leisurely day is spent with family. *Annandag jul*, the day after Christmas, is often spent visiting or entertaining friends.

(MORE THAN) SEVEN KINDS OF COOKIES

Spritz

by Ester Harkins

1 cup butter (do not use margarine)
1/2 cup sugar
1 egg yolk
6 blanched bitter almonds, ground fine (or 1 scant teaspoon almond extract)
2-1/2 cups flour

Preheat oven to 350°. Work the butter and sugar until creamy and fluffy. Mix in the egg yolk. Add the almonds and flour and mix thoroughly. Dough should be quite stiff but still able to pass through a cookie press.

With a cookie press, shape circles or S shapes onto a lightly greased cookie sheet. Bake until golden, about 8 minutes.

Dreams *(Drömmar)*

by Ester Harkins

2 cups sugar
1 cup butter
1 cup vegetable oil
1 tablespoon vanilla
3-1/2 to 4 cups flour
1 teaspoon baking powder

Mix in order given. Form the dough into balls about the size of walnuts. Press the center of each one with your finger to make a dent. (May place a dab of strawberry jam in the circle centers if desired.) Bake at 350° on an ungreased cookie sheet until light tan, about 8 to 10 minutes. Watch so they don't burn!

Sour Cream Cookies *(Surgräddskakor)*

These sour cream sugar cookies are known in our family as "Gammie's Christmas cookies," although my grandmother Anna Elge actually kept them on hand all year. Usually she made them round, sprinkled with plain white sugar. At Christmas, they were cut out in bell, star, tree, or reindeer shapes and sprinkled with multicolored sugars.

2 cups sugar
1 cup shortening
1 egg
1 teaspoon vanilla
1 cup sour cream
2 teaspoons baking soda
approximately 5 cups white flour
plain or colored sugar

Preheat oven to 325°. Mix the sugar and shortening together well; beat in the egg, vanilla, and sour cream. Mix the baking soda with 1 cup flour and stir into the mix, then add the remaining flour, mixing well. Roll the dough out, a little at a time, on a floured board. Sprinkle the top with either plain or colored sugar and roll very lightly to set. Cut out shapes with a cookie cutter and place on a lightly greased cookie sheet. Bake about 10 to 12 minutes until the edges barely begin to brown.

Oatmeal Cookies *(Havrekakor)*

by Anna Elge, my grandmother

1 cup shortening
1 cup sugar
2 eggs
4 tablespoons milk
1 teaspoon vanilla
2 cups flour
1 scant teaspoon baking soda
1 teaspoon baking powder
1 teaspoon cinnamon
1 teaspoon salt
1 cup raisins
2 cups oatmeal

Preheat oven to 375°. Cream the shortening and sugar; mix in the eggs, milk, and vanilla. Combine the flour, baking soda, baking powder, cinnamon, and salt. Stir into the batter. Simmer the raisins in a little water just long enough to soften, then drain. Mix the raisins and oatmeal into the dough. Drop by spoonfuls onto a lightly greased cookie sheet and bake until golden, 10 or 12 minutes.

Nut Logs *(Nötrullar)*

1 stick (1/4 pound) butter or margarine
2/3 cup sugar
1 cup ground pecans
1-2/3 cups flour
chopped pecans

Preheat oven to 400°. Mix shortening and sugar together until smooth and creamy. Add ground nuts and flour and knead together well. Roll into a rope and cut into "logs" of the desired size (should make 10 to 12). Roll each log in chopped nuts, or sprinkle and press them lightly into the surface. For best results, line the cookie sheet with baking paper. Bake about 10 to 12 minutes.

Linking Sweden and America

Architect Tom Blanck of St. Paul, Minnesota, whose ancestors came to Stockholm, Wisconsin, took this snapshot of the Bjurtjam Theatre Group from Värmland, Sweden, in Stockholm in 2004. They also performed at the American Swedish Institute, Minneapolis, and in Willmar and Scandia, Minnesota. The singers, dancers, and actors depicted the life of Erik Peterson, who founded Stockholm, Wisconsin, in 1854. Peterson and his brothers, Petter and Anders, persuaded more than two hundred residents of Sweden to leave for Stockholm, the "paradise on Lake Pepin," part of the Mississippi River.

Crullers *(Klenäter)*

Klenäter *may be translated "poor eats" or "poor man's cookies." Nevertheless, they are tasty enough to be fit for a king.*

6 egg yolks
3 tablespoons sugar
2 tablespoons cream
1/3 cup melted butter or margarine
2 tablespoons brandy
grated peel of 1 lemon
2-1/2 cups flour (approximately)
hot oil for deep-frying
powdered sugar

Beat the egg yolks well. Add the sugar, cream, melted butter, brandy, and lemon peel. Mix very well. Stir in the flour to make a dough the right consistency for rolled cookies. Chill. Roll out very thin. With a pastry cutter or knife, cut the dough into strips about 1-1/2 inches wide, then crosswise or diagonally to make rectangles or diamond shapes about 3 to 4 inches long. Make a lengthwise slit in the middle of each cookie and pull one end through to make a twisted shape. Deep-fry in hot oil (370°) until lightly browned, then drain well on paper towels. When cool, sprinkle with powdered sugar.

Almond Shells *(Mandelmusslor)*

1 cup butter or margarine
3/4 cup sugar
2 egg yolks
2 cups flour
2/3 cup ground almonds

Preheat oven to 350°. Mix the shortening and sugar until smooth and creamy. Mix in the egg yolks, then the flour and ground almonds. Knead until well blended and refrigerate for 1 to 2 hours.

Form the dough into a rope and cut into pieces (should make 3 to 4 dozen). Press each piece into a small, fluted tartlet tin. Bake for 10 to 12 minutes. Turn out of tins while still warm.

Serve plain or filled with jam, fresh fruit, and whipped cream.

Chocolate Cookies *(Chokladbröd)*

1/2 cup butter
1 cup brown sugar
1 egg, beaten
1/2 cup sour cream
2 squares melted chocolate
1-1/2 cups flour
1/4 teaspoon salt
1/4 teaspoon baking soda
1/4 teaspoon baking powder
1 cup chopped walnuts or pecans

Icing ***(Glasyr)*****:**
1 egg, beaten
1 tablespoon milk
1 teaspoon vanilla
1-3/4 cups powdered sugar
1 square melted chocolate

Preheat oven to 375°. Cream the butter and sugar. Add the egg and sour cream and mix thoroughly. Stir in the melted chocolate. Sift together the dry ingredients. Combine with the butter mixture. Stir in the chopped nuts. Drop by spoonfuls onto a lightly greased cookie sheet. Bake 10 to 12 minutes. Combine icing ingredients; mix well. Frost cookies while still warm.

Photo by Mansor Kia

Author Diana Johnson Kia, center, visits with her mother's cousin, Henny Oldenburg, and Henny's husband, Eskil, in Dalarna, Borlänge, Sweden, in 1999.

HOMEMADE CANDY

The following candy recipes come from Barbro Halvarsson.

Toffee *(Kola)*

1 cup cream
1 cup sugar
1/3 cup corn syrup
2 tablespoons cocoa
1 teaspoon cider vinegar
1 tablespoon butter or margarine, melted
15 to 20 chopped sweet almonds

Line an 8 x 8" baking pan with aluminum foil, then lightly grease the foil surface. Mix cream, sugar, syrup, and cocoa in a small saucepan and place over medium heat. When it begins to boil add the vinegar (to prevent it from becoming sugary).

Simmer, uncovered, about 30 minutes, stirring occasionally. Test by dropping a small amount into cold water; it's ready when it holds together. Stir in the melted butter and almonds. Spread in the pan and allow to cool, then cut into squares. Wrap each piece individually in waxed paper.

Snap Candy *(Knäck)*

3/4 cup cream
3/4 cup corn syrup
3/4 cup sugar
2-1/2 tablespoons chopped sweet almonds
4 tablespoons bread crumbs
1/2 teaspoon baking powder

Mix the cream, syrup, and sugar in a saucepan. Bring to a boil and cook, uncovered, about 30 minutes, stirring occasionally. Near the end of the 30 minutes stir in the almonds, bread crumbs, and baking powder. Test by dropping a small amount into cold water; when it can be formed into a little ball it is ready. Spoon into candy papers (you will need two spoons, one for scraping the candy off the other) and allow to cool. Store in a container with a tight-fitting lid, with waxed paper between each layer.

THE CHRISTMAS FEAST

Christmas Ham *(Julskinka)*

1 (10- to 12-pound) cured ham
1 onion, quartered
10 peppercorns
10 whole allspice
1 to 2 bay leaves

Insert a meat thermometer into the thickest part of the ham, but not touching the bone. Place the ham in a pot and add enough water to cover. Add the onion and spices.

Simmer slowly until meat temperature reaches 165°. Allow approximately 1/2 hour per pound.

Remove the rind; allow to cool. Stock may be used for *dopp i grytan* (dip in the kettle) and/or for boiling sausage.

Jansson's Temptation *(Janssons frestelse)*

5 to 6 medium-sized white potatoes
2 medium-sized onions, sliced
3 tablespoons butter, divided
2 (2-ounce) cans anchovies, or 20 Scandinavian anchovies (use a little of the brine if using Scandinavian type)
1-1/2 cups heavy cream
2 tablespoons bread crumbs

Peel the potatoes and cut into strips as for thin French fries. Sauté the onions in 1 tablespoon butter until soft. Layer the onions, potatoes, and anchovies in a greased baking dish. Press lightly on the surface to level it. Pour the cream over the top. Sprinkle with bread crumbs and dot with remaining butter. Bake about 45 minutes at 425°.

Limpa Bread

Charlotte Anderson says that limpa *is a Swedish word for "loaf." For example,* råglimpa *would mean a loaf of rye bread. In America, however,* limpa *has come to mean a particular kind of bread.*

1 cup milk
3 packets active dry yeast
1-1/4 cups lukewarm water
1-1/2 teaspoons sugar
3 cups white flour
1/2 cup corn syrup (dark or light)
1/4 cup molasses
3/4 teaspoon anise seed
3/4 teaspoon fennel seed
6 tablespoons shortening
grated peel of 1 orange
1-1/2 teaspoons salt
4 cups rye flour

Heat the milk until it is almost, but not quite, boiling, then allow it to cool to lukewarm. Dissolve the yeast in the water; add sugar and the milk. Add the white flour and beat well. Allow this "sponge" to rise for 30 minutes. Meanwhile, combine the syrup, molasses, anise, and fennel seed in a small saucepan; bring to a boil and cook for 1 minute. Stir the shortening into the hot syrup so that it melts, then allow to cool to lukewarm. Mix with the sponge; add the grated orange peel, salt, and rye flour. Turn out onto a floured board and knead well. Add a little more white flour as you knead, if necessary.

Shape into two round loaves and place in greased baking pans. Cover with a cloth and allow to rise in a warm place for an hour or so. Preheat the oven to 400°. Before baking, rub a little butter or margarine over the surface of each loaf. Bake at 400° for 15 minutes, then reduce heat to 350° and continue baking for about another 45 minutes. Remove from the oven and again rub the top of each loaf with butter or margarine.

Opposite: *In the little town of Nusnäs, a craftsperson paints finishing touches on a dala horse for export. In Sweden dala horses are not used for Christmas decorations as they are in America.*

Christmas Rice Pudding *(Julgröt)*

2 quarts water
1 cup uncooked rice
2 tablespoons butter or margarine
5 cups milk
1 teaspoon salt
2 tablespoons sugar
1 blanched, whole almond
cinnamon sugar

Bring the water to a boil; add the rice, stir, and allow to simmer for about 2 minutes. Drain off the water and add the butter. Pour the milk into a double boiler; stir in the salt and sugar and add the rice. Cover. Cook about 2 hours, or until rice is tender and milk is absorbed.

Stir in the single almond. Pour pudding into individual serving dishes. (The almond should not be visible.) Sprinkle with cinnamon sugar. Serve warm or cold, with milk. Serves 8.

Lutfisk (Old-fashioned preparation)

It's interesting to look back on what our predecessors went through, even if not many of us may want to try it today!

4 pounds dried lutfisk
1 pound slaked lime
1 pound washing soda
1 quart lukewarm water
cold water

Cut each piece of fish into two or three pieces. Place in a wooden tub or earthenware crock. Cover with plain, cold water and let stand 4 days, changing the water every day. Remove the fish and scrub them well on both sides with a brush. Drain the tub and wash it out. Cover bottom of tub with a layer of lime. Add a layer of fish, skin side down, and cover with another layer of lime. Continue alternating layers of fish and lime until all fish is in the crock. There should be a final layer of lime on top. Dissolve soda in lukewarm water, then allow to cool. Pour over fish. Add enough cold water to cover completely. Weigh the fish down with a plate or other object to make sure it stays submerged. (Hint: Fill a large tight-lock plastic bag with water and use for a weight.) Let stand for 6 to 7 days. Remove fish; wash crock thoroughly. Rinse fish and return to crock. Cover with fresh, cold water. Let stand for at least 4 to 6 more days, changing the water daily.

Cooked Lutfisk *(Lutfisk)*

Cathy Hart uses this recipe for Stanton, Iowa's, annual feast.

1 large Norwegian cod (5 pounds)
1/2 cup butter
salt and pepper
Sauce:
3/4 cup butter
3/4 cup flour
1-1/2 teaspoons salt
1/4 teaspoon pepper
1 quart whole milk, scalded
horseradish mustard (optional)

Lutfisk: Grease a large pan. Lay cod on the bottom. Melt 1/2 cup butter and pour over fish. Sprinkle with salt and pepper. Bake at 350° for 35 minutes or until tender. Remove all bones. **Sauce:** Melt butter, stir in flour, and cook 2 minutes, stirring to prevent scorching. Add salt and pepper and gradually stir in milk. Cook to thicken. If desired, stir in a bit of horseradish mustard to taste, or serve on the side. Combine sauce with fish just before serving. Serve over mashed potatoes.

THE *SMÖRGÅSBORD*
More than just a sandwich table!

The Swedish word *smörgåsbord* may be literally translated "sandwich table," which hardly describes what we have come to expect of this feast for the eye and the palate. This traditional Swedish "buffet style" meal is especially popular at Christmas, but may be enjoyed at any time during the year.

When setting out a *smörgåsbord*, presentation is very important. The table should be colorful and the food attractively arranged. Here are some suggestions for a real Swedish *smörgåsbord,* which may be quite simple or very elaborate:

Basic fare:

Bread, at least three kinds: white, rye, and crispbread
Cheese, at least three kinds
Pickled herring
Pickled beets
Sweet cucumber pickles
Fresh raw vegetables, such as carrots, celery, radishes, cauliflower, cherry, tomatoes
Fruit salad
Hard-cooked eggs, cut in wedges
Swedish meatballs
Ham slices
Dilled potatoes

Other suggestions:

Smoked herring (Kipper Snacks, available in canned fish section of market)
Liver paté
Boiled shrimp
Lobster
Fish in aspic
Salmon
Sausage
Mushrooms
Caviar
Smoked eel
Omelet with asparagus

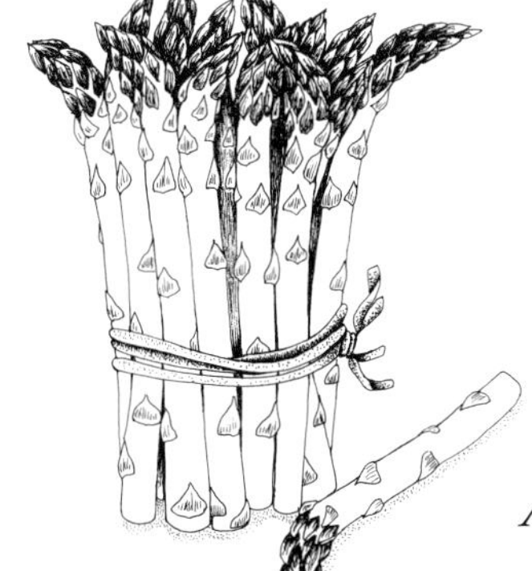

Asparagus

What's for Dinner in Sweden?

The right way to eat a traditional *smörgåsbord*

by Charlotte J. Anderson

The word *smörgåsbord* has become part of the American vocabulary. Contrary to popular belief, it is much more than just a random selection of dishes on a buffet table in its native Sweden.

Sometimes the word is also used to simply explain that you can choose from among several of the items featured in a certain situation — for example, as the *smörgåsbord* of university courses, a *smörgåsbord* of exciting attractions at a tourist spot, or like *USA Today* introduced the Sundance Film Festival, "a smorgasbord [*sic*] of film choices."

The tradition of eating *smörgåsbord* dates back to the early eighteenth century, when it was called "aquavit buffet" *(brännvinsbord).* The sampling of the many dishes, usually an array of herring, Baltic herring, summer sausage, breads, and cheese, was usually consumed while standing, along with shots of aquavit of different flavors. The *smörgåsbord* as such was originally only a buffet of appetizers. When finished, people would take their place at the table, and the main course of the meal would be served.

The type of large-scale *smörgåsbord* you can find throughout Scandinavia today came about in the nineteenth century when the custom spread through established restaurants in the cities and also in railroad restaurants, where the self-serve buffet-style dinners fast became very popular. At this point the tradition also changed so that the *smörgåsbord* buffet offered a whole grand meal featuring not only appetizers but also main courses and desserts.

So, ready to dig in? Well, just hold off for a minute. You'll enjoy Scandinavian food much more if you follow a few simple rules in approaching the dinner buffet. Just as a classic French or Italian meal has a prescribed number and order of courses, a true *smörgåsbord* is best enjoyed in proper order:

Plate 1

Take a plate and approach the part of the *smörgåsbord* where different kinds of herrings are offered. Make your choice from the pickled herrings of many kinds, hard-boiled eggs with or without caviar or cod roe, herring beet root salad, smoked Baltic herring, sour cream, a few small, boiled potatoes, a piece of crispbread with butter and cheese. No meatballs on this plate, please!

Plate 2

On a new plate, sample the different salmon dishes (smoked, pickled, cold, poached, etc.), shrimps, mussels, some mayonnaise, and dill mustard sauce for the salmon (*gravlax* sauce). Yes, you can have another boiled potato and some more bread; the hardtack/crispbread is still very right. However, skip the meatballs this round, too.

Plate 3

Time to approach some meats, but stick with the cold cuts, such as cold roast beef, boiled ham, smoked ham, and different kinds of brawn *(sylta).* Veal brawn is especially popular and well liked. Liver paté and other kinds of paté belong in this round as well, as does the smoked eel, if you'd like to have some more fish. Cold vegetable salads, such as different kinds of pickles and cucumber salads, tomato salad, green salad, radishes, marinated leek, and mustards and other sauces—for example, cumberland sauce—are also enjoyed during round three. A potato? Sure. Some more bread? Sure. Meatballs? NO, not yet.

Plate 4

Ready? Yes, this time around you can try the Swedish meatballs along with other hot dishes! Jansson's Temptation (a casserole with shredded potatoes, anchovies, onions, and cream) is another Swedish favorite. Miniature sausages, minced beef a la Lindström, baked or creamed spinach, baked vegetables, peas, omelette with creamed mushrooms or asparagus, and perhaps a slice of a roast. Potatoes and bread can be enjoyed again, if you still have room. And soon comes round five!

Plate 5

Still hungry? Well, for those with a sweet tooth, that is usually not a problem when it comes to dessert time. The *smörgåsbord* dessert table usually includes a variety of lighter desserts, such as fruit salads, small cookies, different kinds of soft cheeses, and fresh fruits. And, of course, a cup of really strong Swedish coffee to top it off.

To be able to savor the dishes the way they were intended you have to give yourself time, but doesn't that apply to all finer dining? And, if you try to run hundreds of people through a *smörgåsbord* line in an hour, or give people an hour for their meal on board a cruise ship between ports, it is just not going to be according to etiquette.

There are no two *smörgåsbords* alike. Each family can add their touch to the dishes included, and there might be seasonal or regional differences.

A *smörgåsbord* can offer the dinner guests ten, twenty-five, fifty, or one hundred dishes to sample. The brave eater tries only things he can't get at home or hasn't tried before. Kids might stick with meatballs and bread. In Sweden one of the most famous inns, Spångens Gästgivaregård, with a well-known, huge, delicious *smörgåsbord,* has been in business since 1846. Most cruise ships between the Scandinavian countries offer *smörgåsbord* buffet dinners. A *smörgåsbord* experience in Scandinavia is something to remember, a culinary feast for many senses.

Charlotte J. Anderson is originally from Sweden and now lives in Lindsborg, Kansas. She has a degree in communications from the University of Karlstad, Sweden. Charlotte has worked at the National Swedish Radio and has also done free-lance projects for Swedish Television. She is interested in folk traditions and customs and is an experienced instructor of Swedish folk dance and fiddling. Charlotte and her husband, Dean, have two bilingual, bicultural daughters. They own and manage Anderson Butik as well as Anderson Scandinavian Tours.

Pickled Herring *(Inlagd sill)*

Nothing beats the taste of homemade pickled herring.

3 whole salt herring
10 whole allspice
10 whole cloves
10 whole peppercorns
4 bay leaves, crumbled
1 red onion, sliced thin
1/2 cup cider vinegar
1/4 cup water
3/4 cup sugar

Fillet the fish. Soak overnight in water. Next day, drain and cover the fish with fresh water. Soak for several more hours, changing the water several times. Drain and pat dry thoroughly with paper towels.

Cut into serving-sized pieces and place in a bowl. Sprinkle with spices and arrange onion slices on top.

Combine vinegar, water, and sugar and pour this over the fish. Make sure the liquid covers the fish. Cover and refrigerate at least 48 hours.

Pickled Beets *(Inlagda rödbetor)*

small, fresh beets
2 cups vinegar
2 cups water plus more to cover
2 cups sugar

Scrub beets. Place in a large pot, cover with water, and cook until tender. Drain. Cut off stems and tails; skin will slip off. Place beets in hot, sterilized canning jars.

Combine the vinegar, 2 cups water, and sugar and bring to a boil. Pour this liquid over the beets. Seal the jars.

Sweet Cucumber Pickles I *(Syltgurka)*

From Mamrelund Cook Book, Tried & True, *Women's Missionary Society, Stanton, Iowa, 1925*

50 small cucumbers
1/2 cup salt
cold water
2 cups vinegar
1/2 cup water
4 cups sugar
2 teaspoons celery seed
2 teaspoons mustard seed
2 teaspoons allspice
1 teaspoon black pepper

Alternate layers of cucumbers and salt in a pan. Add cold water and let stand overnight. In the morning, drain off water but do not rinse off the salt.

Mix the remaining ingredients in a saucepan. Bring to a boil and simmer for 5 minutes. Add the prepared cucumbers and let stand for 15 minutes. Pack in jars and fill with the liquid. Seal. Store in a cold, dark place.

Sweet Cucumber Pickles II *(Syltgurka)*

From Mamrelund Cook Book, Volume II, Tried & True, *Ladies' Aid Society, Stanton, Iowa, 1935*

7 pounds cucumbers
brine solution (1/2 cup coarse salt for every 4 cups water)
7 cups vinegar, divided
3 quarts plus 1 cup water, divided
1 tablespoon powdered alum
3 pounds sugar
1 teaspoon cinnamon
1 tablespoon celery seed
1 tablespoon whole allspice

Peel the cucumbers. Cover with brine solution and soak for 3 days. Drain and cover with fresh water. Let stand for another 3 days, changing water daily. Cut cucumbers in chunks. Place in a large pot and add 4 cups vinegar, 3 quarts water, and alum. Bring to a boil. Turn off heat and allow to cool for an hour. Bring to a boil again. Drain and place pickles in hot, sterilized jars.

Combine sugar, cinnamon, celery seed, and allspice. Place spices in a bag. Place the spice bag in a pot along with 3 cups vinegar and 1 cup water. Bring to a boil and simmer for a few minutes. Pour over pickles in jars and seal immediately.

Dilled Potatoes *(Kokt potatis med dill)*

small, red potatoes, preferably new potatoes
water
salt
butter or margarine
fresh, chopped dill

Peel the potatoes. Place in a pot and add water and a little salt. Simmer until tender, approximately 30 minutes. Drain. Melt butter and drizzle over the potatoes. Chop the dill and sprinkle over the potatoes. Toss lightly. Transfer to a serving bowl.

Note: If fresh dill is not available, use a little dry dill weed spice.

Liver Paté *(Leverpastej)*

1 pound chicken livers
1 pound ground sirloin
4 ounces lean smoked ham, minced
1 large onion, finely chopped
2 cloves garlic, minced
2 eggs
1/2 cup flour
1/2 cup heavy cream
salt, pepper, and oregano to taste
2 tablespoons cognac

Rinse, dry, and grind the chicken livers. Mix with the sirloin and ham. Add the onion and garlic. In a separate bowl, mix the eggs, flour, and cream and fold into the meat mixture. Add the seasonings and cognac. Place in a greased, oblong oven dish, cover with aluminum foil, and bake at 350° for 1-1/2 hours. Allow to cool completely before serving.

Fish in Aspic *(Fiskaladåb)*

4 cups water
1 tablespoon lemon juice
2 teaspoons salt
5 peppercorns
5 allspice
2 bay leaves
dill sprigs
1/2 cup grated carrot
2 pounds salmon or eel

For the aspic:
2 tablespoons gelatin
2 cups cold fish stock
2 egg whites
salt
pepper

Combine water, lemon juice, spices, and carrot and simmer 20 minutes. Clean and skin fish and cut into pieces. Add fish to stock; simmer another 10 to 15 minutes until fish is cooked but not falling apart. Carefully remove fish from stock, separate meat from bones, and set aside. Discard bones. Allow stock to cool completely.

Dissolve gelatin in the cold stock, add egg whites, and beat well. Bring stock to a boil, stirring constantly, then remove from heat; cover, and let stand for 15 minutes. Strain the stock well. Season to taste with salt and pepper.

Pour about 1/3 of the aspic liquid into a mold and chill until set. Add cold fish pieces to the mold and pour in the remaining aspic. Chill until set.

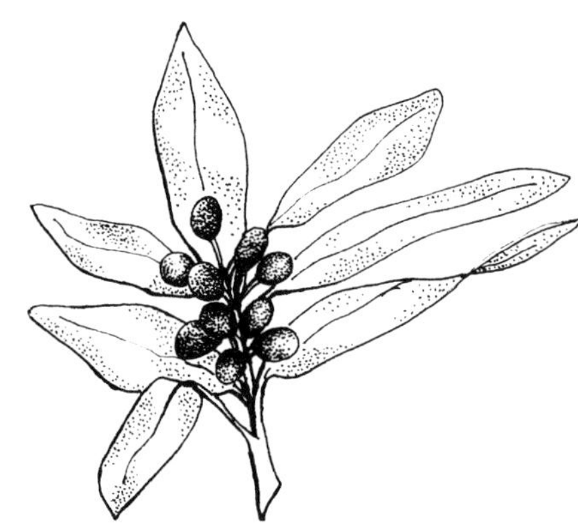

Bay leaves

Listing of Recipes

Remembering Sweden

Viking Stone near Göteborg (Gothenburg)

Gripsholm's Castle in Sörmland

Harbor at Bohuslän

Lappland
Sweden
Norrbotten
Jämtland
Västerbotten
Ångermanland
Härjedalen
Medelpad
Dalama
Hälsingland
Värmland
Gästrikland
Bohuslän
Dalsland
Västmanland
Närke
Uppland
Västergötland
Södermanland
Halland
Östergötland
Småland
Skåne
Blekinge
Öland
Gotland